HOW TO DEVELOP, INSTALL, AND MAINTAIN A COST REDUCTION/PRODUCTIVITY IMPROVEMENT PROGRAM

Raymond J. Behan

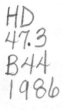 VAN NOSTRAND REINHOLD COMPANY
——————————————————————— New York

Copyright © 1986 by Van Nostrand Reinhold Company Inc.

Library of Congress Catalog Card Number: 83-1299
ISBN: 0-442-21280-1

Manufactured in the United States of America

Published by Van Nostrand Reinhold Company Inc.
135 West 50th Street, New York, N.Y. 10020

Macmillan of Canada
Division of Gage Publishing Limited
164 Commander Boulevard
Agincourt, Ontario M1S 3C7, Canada

Van Nostrand Reinhold
480 Latrobe Street
Melbourne, Victoria 3000, Australia

Van Nostrand Reinhold Company Limited
Molly Millars Lane
Workingham, Berkshire RG11 2PY, England

15 14 13 12 11 10 9 8 7 6 5 4 3 2 1

Library of Congress Cataloging in Publication Data

Behan, Raymond J.
  How to develop, install, and maintain a cost reduction/productivity improvement program.

  Includes index.
  1. Cost control.   2. Industrial productivity.
I. Title.
HD47.3.B44   1986   658.1'552   83-1299
ISBN 0-442-21280-1

*To my wife, Ellen, without whose untiring efforts,
this book would never have reached completion*

HOW TO DEVELOP, INSTALL, AND MAINTAIN A COST REDUCTION/PRODUCTIVITY IMPROVEMENT PROGRAM

Preface

Over the past twenty plus years, I have had the opportunity to conduct analyses for profit improvement potential in more than three hundred organizations including manufacturing companies, banks, insurance companies, hospitals, refineries, oil and gas production, utilities, hotel chains, and four universities.

The ultimate result of the great majority of these analyses is the revelation that each organization has failed to fully utilize their available resources. For the most part, the reason is very simple: they do not know how optimize these resources, including human, and as a result have large, open, unused capacity. This holds true in organizations of all sizes and types regardless of the sophistication of their operations.

For example, in the engineering department of a large New England manufacturer, which was using a very sophisticated computerized scheduling system, the analysis revealed that they were losing 8 man weeks per week of the engineers' time. This represented about 18% of the engineering work force. They were expending overtime hours to make up their deficit. Yet, the fact was not recognized— very commonplace situation.

Even in many organizations where the problem has been recognized, at least in broad terms, the ability to take effective corrective action is often nullified by the day-by-day activity of just keeping the business going. The head nurse of a large hospital once commented on how much of the busy work of the ancillary personnel, to her amazement, was being done by the nursing staff. This, after an analysis that revealed the amount of open capacity among the ancillary group.

During this same period of time, I was privileged to direct the efforts of several hundred companies and, within those companies, many more hundreds of departments in the development of programs that increased resource utilization many times over. The cost reduction/profit improvement techniques described in this book were maturing rapidly. The state of the art continuously improves. Many consulting firms, as well as the consulting arms of a number of the larger accounting firms in the country have utilized some of these techniques, and do so today, contributing to the growth and profitability of numerous organizations. I continue to develop and manage programs to accomplish such results.

Out of these experiences came the realization of the need for a book that could *instruct* companies on how to *develop, install* and *maintain* a program that would accomplish the improvements which appear to be so essential for their health and well-being. Why the need? Certainly, if in my own experience, the need is overwhelmingly evident, then how many more companies would benefit?

Many firms, over the years, have employed the services of consultants such as myself, and will continue to do so, for we do have a catalytic value and the ability to pursue this type of goal within the company without the responsibility of running the daily affairs of the business. However, there are not enough consultants in the world to reach all of the firms that could benefit from such techniques. Additionally, many firms may not be of a size or financial position to afford consulting services of this kind. *Yet, they all have a need.*

What better way to give these firms, through their own people, the ability to accomplish profit improvements than to produce a book that contains step by step instructions on how to enhance their profitability through instituting a program designed specifically for that purpose? It is believed that this has been accomplished.

Who should read this book? The executive? . . . Yes, because executive decision making will be enhanced by the information contained in the book. Middle managers? . . . Yes, because they are in a position to contribute to profit improvement in the most direct manner. Supervisors? . . . Yes, since it is their areas of responsibility that the impact of any profit improvement program will be most felt.

A strong readership should develop among students of management. The principles, methods and techniques in this book would certainly enhance their management education. Developing the ability to analyze operations for improvement potential, in itself, increases the value of a promotional candidate a hundredfold.

But this book is not written merely for reading; it is written for *applying*. There is no greater satisfaction for an author than to see his thoughts in print and I've been looking forward to that. However, to come across a firm that has completely installed and is maintaining such a program as the result of this book—that will be the ultimate feeling of *MISSION ACCOMPLISHED*.

RAYMOND J. BEHAN

Contents

HOW TO DEVELOP, INSTALL, AND MAINTAIN A COST REDUCTION/PRODUCTIVITY IMPROVEMENT PROGRAM

1
Introduction

This book is designed to provide the basis for developing a cost reduction/productivity improvement program in most types of companies. It will help channel an organization's efforts in a constructive fashion toward recognizing the existing opportunities for cost reduction/productivity improvement and toward approaching these opportunities in a planned manner.

Drastic inflation, lack of productivity improvements, and the declining value of the dollar led to a great deal of emphasis on developing new technologies to cope with these problems. Technological development made and continues to make dramatic impact on the way we manufacture, communicate, ship and receive, process information, use our labor and other resources, and dispose of our waste products. This book is not concerned with technology, however. It is a compilation of common-sense principles of sound management practice.

The terms *cost reduction* and *profit improvement* will be used interchangeably throughout the book. Though there are differences in actual meaning, the result being sought is an improved bottom line. Unless the results can be measured in real dollars, they become academic. Another term that could be applied is *cost avoidance,* but it refers to the future and has a bearing on long-range results. We, on the other hand, are dealing with the here and now.

THE REQUIREMENT OF COMPLETE INVOLVEMENT

What most companies *can* do and *should* do, if they are to fully succeed in reducing costs, slowing cost increases, and improving

1

profitability, is to develop a complete internal program that will involve the entire organization in the effort. The program must be permanent and ongoing. It must have structure and substance, goals to achieve, and a plan to achieve those goals. It must deal with improving the productive effort of all facets of the operation.

Several years ago, one of the larger motel chains in the United States found itself in deep trouble. Increased costs were driving them out of their budget-luxury status. They employed a consultant to help them reduce costs. Within a year, the bottom line was considerably improved, but more important, they realized that a permanent program would be required if they were to maintain and improve their gains. The job of organizing and leading the program was given to a corporate vice president as his sole responsibility. Through his continued effort, the chain is now one of the most profitable in the country and a leader in providing good, clean accommodations at a most reasonable cost to the traveling public. They still use consultants as the need arises to give them a particular direction but under the control of the program vice president.

ACTIVE PARTICIPATION BUT NOT INTERFERENCE

To be successful, the program, from day one of its planning, must be regarded as a permanent part of the company's philosophy of doing business. One-shot, hard-hitting efforts can have immediate (if sometimes painful) results. The program must be developed in detail, properly structured throughout the organization, and have its own lines of responsibility and communication. It must *not* interfere with, nor be designed to replace, legitimate functions of industrial or product engineering, accounting or methods departments, though it may draw upon the expertise of any of these.

The program must be designed to have *active participation* throughout the organization. To accomplish this, it will be necessary to have all levels of management, as well as labor, involved in it. Throughout the book you will see how this can be accomplished.

The full backing of top management will be essential. In some companies, it will be better to have top management actually run the program. In others, the delegation of the operation of the program to a lower echelon may be desirable but the lines of communication to the top must be open.

An example of the problems that can occur when the program is not universal in scope can be found in the experience of a southwestern manufacturing plant. The technical laboratory manager developed a productivity improvement program for his lab. The improvement brought about was very impressive, but the adverse effects on the engineering department were profound. After the lab manager and chief engineer got together, the program was extended to engineering. Again, excellent results were achieved but production and marketing felt adverse repercussions. When the plant manager got into the act, he recognized the benefits, appointed a coordinator, and expanded the program throughout the plant. Full success was achieved, and the program is ongoing. A sense of accomplishment permeated the entire plant. Not only was morale improved, but the total plant cost, as related to units of production, was considerably reduced.

THE NEED TO INCORPORATE *EFFORTS* WITHIN A *PROGRAM*

A program is more than an effort. Many companies have cost control, cost reduction, or profit improvement *efforts* on an ongoing or spot basis. Many either sporadically or regularly employ specialists to attack specific cost areas. Though these *efforts* can be very productive, they should be incorporated into a program, not considered as a program unto themselves.

WORK SCHEDULING AS A KEY ELEMENT

A key element in a meaningful productivity improvement program is the scheduling of work on a short-interval basis. Most companies have some means of scheduling work. Having determined the needs of the marketplace, companies gear up to provide for them. Manufacturing companies have their production planning functions that, on a broad basis, match the requirements of product to the facility. However, many unnecessary costs get built in because planners, looking at the broad picture, miss necessary ingredients of good work scheduling. Capacities are mismatched. In-process inventories build up. Imbalances and shortages of parts and raw materials occur, and often finished-goods inventories have no relationship to the needs of the marketplace. These factors often go unrecognized and are very costly. A continuous cost reduction/productivity improvement program can bring them under control.

Many years ago, a single-panel cartoon appeared in a newspaper or magazine depicting a cigar-smoking manufacturing manager standing in the middle of a factory floor, holding an order sheet in one hand. With the other hand he was scratching his head as he complained in plaintive tones to a second character: "I just wish the sales department would stop selling the items that I'm out of the parts for!" His dilemma is all too typical of the kind of problems that companies learn to accept as a norm of doing business. Work-scheduling techniques incorporated into a productivity improvement program can continuously monitor and correct this type of situation to minimize production delays, reduce in-process time, and the storage of material and labor in unnecessary inventories.

NONMANUFACTURING ORGANIZATIONS CAN BENEFIT

Service organizations and institutions are not immune to problems of work-flow interruptions, duplication of effort, and failure to control the performance factors required to provide good service. They often lack awareness of basic scheduling techniques to control productivity. As a result, excess costs are built in to compensate for the absence of good management control.

In a Brooklyn, New York, hospital, a study revealed that the nurses were spending up to 40% of their time doing menial tasks that non-professional personnel could perform. As part of the total productivity improvement program, the methods of work assignment were revised. Ancillary personnel were assigned on a scheduled basis and about 75% of the nurses' time devoted to busy work was recaptured and returned to patient care. The hospital was able to roll back its employment program, hire fewer nurses than were previously considered necessary, and provide excellent service at a considerably reduced cost. The same possibilities exist in many institutions and organizations. The growth that takes place—the additional services to customers, the increase in the number of customers to be served, the ever-expanding paper work—occurs at a pace that leaves only minimal opportunity to take a long hard look at the possibilities for developing better, more efficient and less costly procedures. Even the ever-increasing use of computer technology leaves vast opportunity for in-depth examination of the total effort itself and all of the intricate details and activities that comprise the effort. As you will see, the room for reducing costs and improving productivity in the growth areas mentioned is never-ending.

THE NECESSITY OF TRAINING FIRST-LINE SUPERVISORS

Supervisory training in many organizations consists of taking a technically competent person and giving him or her the basics of the philosophy of management and an introduction to the administrative functions of supervision. The program to reduce costs and improve productivity will include the training of supervisors in the management of the resources, both human and material, that are at their disposal. It will make them fully conscious of their role as managers and will provide them with the tools of management.

THE HUMAN RELATIONS ASPECT

In the development of the program, the basic mission, that of improving productivity and reducing costs, is paramount. However, those charged with the conduct of the program must also be fully aware of the human relations aspect of their function. The overall program must fit into the company philosophy of how to deal with the human factor. People must not feel threatened by the program. If a bargaining agreement exists, care must be taken that it is not violated. People are least fearful when they understand the company's goals and the reasons for them.

In embarking on a program to improve productivity, a major northeastern bank held a series of meetings, first for its officers, then for the officers and their supervisors, and finally for the supervisors and their people. The program explanation included the fact that a reduction in the number of personnel was expected to result. It was clearly, and without equivocation, pointed out that no one in the organization would lose his or her job. Personnel reductions would take place only through attrition or promotion. The overall result was, from an employee relations viewpoint, very positive. People became involved in the program and contributed (and continue to contribute) to its success. From a financial point of view, in the several years that the program has been in operation, the hours used per unit of work produced has declined by as much as 31%.

FULL AND DETERMINED COMMITMENT

This book will provide the principles of developing, implementing, and maintaining a cost reduction, productivity improvement program. It will give the reader general fundamentals, specific instructions, anticipated results, and examples of how many companies have successfully used all or some of the principles involved.

The undertaking of a program, be it in total as recommended, or in part to meet a specific situation, should be done with full and determined commitment. It should be approached in a positive, aggressive, and enthusiastic manner. Only in this way can it be expected to produce lasting benefits. To do less would be an injustice that could damage the well being of the organization and the morale of its people.

2

Organizing for the Cost Reduction/ Productivity Improvement Program

The purpose of this chapter is to provide the necessary ingredients of organizational structure to assure a successful program. Inherent in the development of the organizational structure is recognition of responsibility, expectations and limitations, participation and co-operation, and lines of communication. The organization is primary before a program is actually activated. The alternatives in the structuring process will be discussed.

VARIABLES TO CONSIDER

The decision-making process, having concluded that a program will be developed, installed, and maintained on an ongoing basis, must then proceed to the organizing stage. The structure will be dependent on a variety of factors

- The size of the company
- Numbers of departments
- Numbers of people
- Present line of authority
- Degree of autonomy

The best way to proceed is to examine the organization chart of the company in some depth. Look at its breadth as well as its depth. Where, in this structure, is it best to place the responsibility for the development of the program? At this point, we are not considering the ultimate form that the structure will take. What is required is the *point* from which the rest will follow.

The answer will be found in the upper portion of the organization chart. Look for the *lowest* ranking senior officer whose authority and responsibility encompasses the entire organization that is to come under the program. This could be an executive vice president, the chief financial officer, vice president of manufacturing, vice president for administration, and in some instances the company president. The responsibility to be assigned that officer will be to create the organization, define the goals, establish basic procedures, and set priorities among the targets for improvement. If he is not to *command* the program, he must select, from somewhere in the organization, that person who will be the program leader or coordinator.

SELECTING THE RIGHT PERSON FOR COORDINATION

It is important that the right person be selected for the position. The position of coordinator is the liaison between management and the various departments. Here are some guidelines for the selection process.

The candidate should be:

- Company and management oriented
- Cost conscious and objective
- Enthusiastic in nature; aggressive without being abrasive
- Confident in carrying out duties
- A firm believer in achieving company goals
- Strong in understanding human relations
- Personable, service minded, with a liking for planning and directing

At this point, the candidate sounds like a combination of Jack Armstrong and Albert Schweitzer with a little bit of Superman thrown in. Where can such a person be found?

Within the organization, the type of person can usually be found in the ranks of middle management or at the level of supervisor. The person sought will have already achieved recognition as a *promotional candidate.* He or she will be respected by his or her peers and superiors. The person will have fair to good knowledge of overall company operations and a willingness to learn more. It will be someone who has made himself or herself known as a dependable individual who has consistently put out more than what was expected.

Conversely, the person should *not be selected* merely on the basis that he or she has time available or the position currently filled is vague or innocuous in its importance, or can be reduced in scope or eliminated. The person should not be one who has already achieved his or her level of competence and who has been happily ensconced in one little niche over a protracted period. Mainly, keep in mind that if the program is to be successful, this individual will be the key to that success. Keep in mind also that the one filling this position will, in most instances, learn so much about the company's operations and develop such in-depth understanding of company goals and objectives that he or she will become a most valuable player on the management team.

THE UPWARD CAREER PATH OF COORDINATORS

Five years after being selected as the coordinator for his bank's cost reduction program, one individual became the administrative vice president of the bank. Another program coordinator in a manufacturing plant became the plant manager in a year and a half, beating out candidates who were older and had been in middle management for several years. A number of coordinators have developed their skills to the degree that they now work as consultants in applying cost reduction techniques in companies completely unrelated to their prior work experience.

DUTIES OF THE COORDINATOR

The coordinator function will be multifaceted and will have very specific duties, which will include:

- The development of the program
- Establishment of initial goals
- Scheduling the activities of the program
- Holding meetings with managers and supervisors

- Directing the efforts of other people on specific assignments within given areas of application
- Following up on problems
- Assuring the implementation of all aspects of the program
- Recording and reporting results

The situation described above is a "one person show." The coordinator will start out by doing an analysis of all of the departments and subsections within the company. (See Chapter 3.) From the information developed, the coordinator will lay out a schedule of achievement and will proceed to develop the program. He or she will have the authority to place requirements on management and supervision to take specific steps and will have the full backing of top management.

One of the country's major theme parks, deeply involved in a cost reduction program, found its program floundering for lack of coordination. The initial approach was to have a coordinator in each of the departments. Management ran into problems because *overall* coordination was missing, and so selected a woman from the food service department, more for her personality and cost-conscious thinking than for her specific background. Her reporting level was to the corporate controller whose authority superseded even the park manager. Within three months she pulled the program into line. By six months, the savings achieved exceeded all expectations. After two years, the program continues to produce benefits far in excess of the cost of operating it.

HOW SOME COMPANIES IMPLEMENT SUCCESSFUL PROGRAMS

The larger the company, the more people may be required to operate a successful program. In developing the structure, consideration must be given to the cost-benefit ratio. In the hotel chain mentioned in Chapter 1, the program coordination effort shaped up as shown in Exhibit 2.1.

Since the program had to be developed, installed, and operated on a continuous basis in over 100 motels with results reported daily, it was necessary to have a staff of four people. The annual cost ran about $150,000. The savings in the first year approached two million dollars. An additional savings of over one million dollars occurred

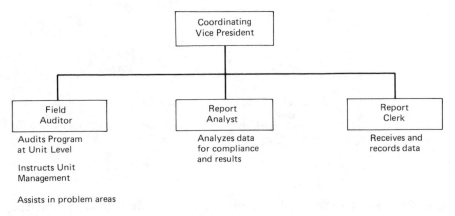

Exhibit 2–1.

in the second year. The program in its fourth year continues to justify the cost as the staff works diligently on a daily basis to assure its perpetuation. The cost proved to be a small price to pay for the results that are being attained.

One large manufacturing organization with over 200 plants around the world has implemented programs in more than 30 plants within 2 years. Each plant has a full-time coordinator who assures that the areas within the plant currently participating continue to do so. The coordinator also has the responsibility to expand the program to all areas within the plant. Because of the size and scope of the program, the company uses a major consulting firm to assist in developing and implementing the program in each plant and to train the coordinators.

At the upper levels, the coordination is accomplished through regional executives to whom the plant coordinator reports on a direct line. Exhibit 2.2 shows how this occurs.

Another type of structure dispenses with the position of coordinator and places the function in the hands of department managers. Each manager's job description contains a specific charge to continue to maintain and improve the ongoing profit improvement program.

One New England manufacturer has such a structure in its plant. The responsibility is pyramided along the direct reporting lines within the company up to the level of the executive vice president who re-

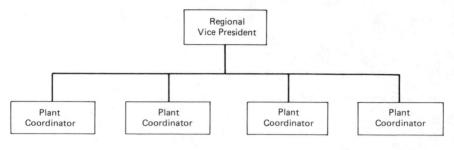

Exhibit 2–2.

ports weekly to the president on the results for the week and the plans for the coming week as related to the program.

Some organizations operate the program through a committee. This approach has the advantage of utilizing a variety of talents from the organization. The committee can have a permanent chairman and several permanent members with temporary chairs occupied by a representative of one or more departments as the program is developed and implemented in those departments. In taking the committee approach, it is essential that the committee *chairman* reports directly to an officer of the company whose position is high enough to have broad influence, if not direct lines of authority, over most, if not all, of the operation. The chairman is, in effect, the program coordinator.

The committee approach can be most successful in the smaller company, particularly one that cannot afford the luxury of a full-time coordinator. Care must be taken, however, that the committee operates within the boundaries of specific guidelines. It is all too easy to have one committee member, whose dominant personality overshadows others, channel the effort in a singular fashion and neglect many good opportunities for productivity improvement. Care must also be exercised that the activity of the committee has a high priority. Members must participate fully, attend meetings, and carry out designated assignments.

THE CENTRAL IMPORTANCE OF STRUCTURING EMPLOYEE EXPECTATIONS

As you will see in a later chapter, a continuous reporting procedure, though only a tool to relay information, is essential to a successful program. But what people do with the information is the really important point. A program structure must be in place for the reporting procedure to work properly. Still, it is necessary to develop the program *around* people. Most people function best in a reasonably structured environment. When people understand what is expected of them, and those expectations are not beyond their ability to perform, they usually function well. If the expectations are insufficient, performance will adjust to the lower level. So in organizing for a good productivity improvement program, give every consideration to the goals to be established, the approach meeting those goals, and the requirements that will be placed on people as a result.

ADDITIONAL ALTERNATIVES

There are a number of alternatives that present themselves as possible ways to organize for productivity improvement. Keep in mind that the purpose is to organize for a long-range, permanent program that is expected to be perpetuated ad infinitum.

First, look at the single coordinator function and raise questions related to the ability of one person to accomplish the goals of the program, either on a part-time or full-time basis.

How long will it take one person to analyze the operation in sufficient depth to establish the framework of the program? As shown in Chapter 3, this symptomatic analysis should be quite comprehensive.

Assume that the analysis will demonstrate considerable savings potential. With what degree of alacrity does the company want to exploit that potential?

Will the single coordinator be able to draw on the time of people in the organization to perform the necessary tasks? How much supervisory time in various departments can be put to work on the program under the coordinator's direction?

Is the company willing to go to the outside for the talent required to "attack," develop, and implement portions of the program (consulting specialists)?

The answers to the above questions will assist in determining whether or not the single-coordinator approach will be feasible. Keep in mind that the initial expectations can be overwhelming for one person unless the person can draw on others for specific assistance in the program development. The alternative would be to only achieve small results gradually over a long period. Recognize that the maintenance of the program, once it is in full operation, will require a lot less effort than its initial development and implementation. The impact of the initial implementation can be very lucrative and dramatic whereas the long-range benefits, though increasingly beneficial, will be less dramatic. Once the program has permeated the organization, it becomes easier to manage, and one person should be able to handle it in single-location companies of moderate size.

Expanding to a multicoordinator function, or actually starting out with several coordinators, can accomplish results more quickly. This is particularly true if the size of the organization is either too large or too complex for one person. The problem presented in this situation is simply one of coordinating the coordinators. The solution is to have a supercoordinator who will have overall responsibility and to whom the others will report. Unlike the committee approach, this becomes an organizational structure of its own. Care must be exercised in its development within the organization so as to avoid conflict with lines of authority already in place. The supercoordinator will be devoted full time to the program. Others may be drawn from various parts of the organization, but a percentage of their time must be *committed* to the program. An alternative to the multicoordinator function would be a coordinating department. It is possible that the function can be domiciled in an existing department such as methods and procedures, or, in the case of a manufacturing organization, the industrial engineering department or the production control department. A number of companies have successfully operated a productivity improvement program in this manner.

One of the pitfalls of this approach is that the program can take a low priority in the overall responsibilities of the department. To be successful, the program *must have a high priority*. Evidence of this can be seen when a company hires a consultant to come in and develop an entire program. The consultant will not normally operate in an environment that does not give top priority to the program. Many instances can be demonstrated where the effort failed for this reason.

A large baking company hired a consulting organization to implement a productivity improvement program in one of its bakeries in an eastern city. Having accepted the assignment, the consultants found themselves in an environment where their assigned work space was little more than a storage closet, the plant manager was too busy to give them the necessary time, and the selected coordinator was continuously drawn off on other matters deemed more important. In a very short period of time, it became clear throughout the plant that the program was not regarded as particularly important. Department heads dragged their feet and actually competed with the consultants, attacking their credibility from all angles. Needless to say, the program fell short of expectations and almost failed completely. Only the efforts of the president of the division prevented a disaster.

USE OF A COORDINATING OFFICE

Where the potential for profit improvement warrants the expense, a coordinating office can be established, consisting of a manager and whatever staff is required. The size and nature of the staff would be determined by the scope of the program. It should be large enough to develop and install the program in a reasonable length of time and to maintain it on a long-range basis. Such a department must be continuously challenged with opportunities to expand its efforts, either through its own dynamic and aggressive seeking, or through continuous input from other departments, or a combination. It must not be allowed to assume functions not directly related to the program, nor should such functions be demanded of it. Instances can be cited where such a department, once the program was firmly established and well underway, was able to assume additional responsibilities. These are exceptional cases that tend to dilute the effort. Where the coordinating office has worked most successfully, it has kept the running of the program as its primary mission.

REVIEW AND DECIDE

A number of structures have been discussed. A decision as to the best structure for any particular company will depend on a number of factors. Which structure will fit?

- Single coordinator
- Several coordinators
- Independent coordinating function

- Coordinating function domiciled in an existing office
- Committee organization
- Domiciling responsibility within the present management function

Whichever approach is selected, it should fit the structure and nature of the host organization. Approaches can be changed and the structure redefined if necessary. The most important factor is to get started in an organized fashion.

Up to this point, two important decisions must have been made.

1. A productivity improvement program will be implemented.
2. An organizational structure to develop and implement the program has been put in place.

It is now time to define the program through an in-depth analysis of the operations.

3

Analysis for Cost Reduction/ Productivity Improvement Potential

The program for cost reduction/productivity improvement will be most successful if all areas are subjected to an analysis that will define the potential and enable a schedule to be made and goals to be set. The analysis will be similar to a physician's examination of a patient. It will be designed to assess those symptoms that indicate the need for remedial action.

ANALYZING THE SYMPTOMS

The methodology will basically be a threefold approach.

- Interviews with those people closest to each operation
- Review of historical records
- Observations of current activities

From these simple steps, it is possible to develop enough symptomatic data upon which to base decisions relative to developing the program.

WHERE TO START

It is best to start in those areas that are labor intensive. An examination of the organizational structure and payroll records can usually reveal which areas incur the highest costs. Once these are defined in terms of size, the analysis can be started. This chapter will be devoted to the methods of analysis as they apply to the various areas in general and to specific types of analysis that can be applied to individual operations.

INTERVIEWS WITH DEPARTMENT MANAGERS AND SUPERVISORS

The inverview technique is designed to determine just how much information the manager and the supervisor have at their command that enables them to manage the resources for which they are responsible. It will further develop how they use the data in the day-by-day function of control. The results will go a long way toward revealing the potential degree of improvement that is available through the development of productivity improvement techniques. The interview will also develop information on the managers' or supervisors' attitudes, how they perceive their problems, and indeed what some of the problems are that detract from the ability of the department to produce.

HOW TO CONDUCT THE INTERVIEW

The interview should start with the top manager of the department and proceed, under his direction, through the supervisory levels down to the first line supervisor. The interviews should be held in the office or work area of the person being interviewed since this is where that person will be most at ease. The manner should be friendly and relaxed, and convey the feeling that the interviewer desires to help that person to improve his or her situation. The more informal the better.

Since the interviewer will, in most instances, be relatively unfamiliar with the specifics of the area, a good way to start is to have the manager or supervisor explain the function of the department or section. This has a settling influence since it is an easy subject for that person to discuss and will open the door for conversation.

The person doing the interviewing should be realistically interested in what the other has to say. This is not a difficult stance to take since the outcome of the interview will substantially affect the position of the department in the program.

INTERVIEWING THE MANAGER

An overall picture of a department that has supervisors between management and the work force should be obtained from the manager. The following information should be sought:

- An overview of the department and its function
- How the department is organized to accomplish the function (full details on the structure of the department, down to the last person in it)
- Knowledge of the work input, flow-through and output of the department and subsections
- Deadline requirements for work output

The key to the management interview, as it relates to the potential for cost savings, is how much knowledge the manager has of the volume of work and how well he has related to it the work force, equipment, and other necessary resources. Are records of input available? Records of output? Records of hours worked? Are the volume records compared to the hours worked? Is there a goal(s) of accomplishment based on some kind of unit of work production? How well are the goals met? How were they established? Are the goals monthly, weekly, daily? Are records kept? Pick up samples of available records.

How was the staffing in the department established? Are there *specific* yardsticks to relate the number of people to the work volume? What are they? Again, pick up samples of any records.

Does the manager receive reports directly from his supervisors on work output, backlogs, schedule conditions, problems? Are these formal reports with documentation? How often are they received? Are they kept in a file? Ask for copies of reports for at least the past several weeks.

How does the manager rate his supervisors? Does he have clear-cut, objective yardsticks related to the performance that is measurable? Are these ongoing? How are they used to improve supervisory performance? Ask for a specific example and copies of any documentation.

Exhibit 3.1 is a chart designed to enable the interviewer to rate the

MANAGEMENT INTERVIEW SUMMARY

	YES	NO
DOES HE HAVE ACCURATE RECORDS OF:		
WORK INPUT?	☐	☐
WORK OUTPUT?	☐	☐
HOURS WORKED?	☐	☐
BACKLOG?	☐	☐
DOES HE HAVE ESTABLISHED **GOALS** TO ACCOMPLISH		
WEEKLY?	☐	☐
DAILY?	☐	☐
HOURLY?	☐	☐
DOES HE RELATE HOURS WORKED TO UNITS PRODUCED?	☐	☐
DOES HE KNOW HOW THE NUMBER OF PEOPLE IN HIS DEPARTMENT WAS ESTABLISHED?	☐	☐
DOES HE RECEIVE REPORTS FROM HIS SUPERVISORS		
WEEKLY?	☐	☐
DAILY?	☐	☐
DOES HE KNOW HIS SCHEDULE STATUS AT ALL TIMES?	☐	☐
DOES HE HAVE OBJECTIVE CRITERIA TO RATE HIS SUPERVISORS?	☐	☐

EACH YES ANSWER HAS POINT VALUE OF 1

RATING

EXCELLENT	GOOD	FAIR	POOR
12–14	9–11	7–10	under 7

Exhibit 3–1.

manager's replies as related to the *degree* of *control* he has over his department. The rating of the interviewer with the manager is one of *probability*. The lower the score, the more probability exists for improvement potential. In most instances, the higher-scoring manager has better control, reducing, but not eliminating the potential. It is important to secure documentation, as indicated earlier, and to evaluate it. The distinction must be made between the manager who says (and believes) that he is in control and the one who actually is.

With the management interview completed, the stage is set to interview those supervisors below the manager.

Special note: If the manager is the direct supervisor of the work force (i.e., does not have supervisory positions between himself and the workers) the supervisory interview technique should be used.

INTERVIEWING THE SUPERVISOR

The supervisor should have the most intimate knowledge of the workings of his or her department or section. The line of questioning involved is designed to determine just how much knowledge he or she has of the productive output of the people and how well their time is utilized on a day-to-day or even hour-to-hour basis. The less knowledge demonstrated by the supervisor, the higher the probability that there is room for increasing the productivity of the work area.

The line of questioning should be conversational. Notes should be taken, particularly of those things that the supervisor feels are needed to improve the situation in the department. The words *productivity, profitability, cost reduction,* and so on are *not* used during the interview. They can draw adverse reactions. The interviewer should not attempt to make suggestions or to ask questions that have any critical implications such as why the supervisor does or does not do things in a particular way.

In the final analysis, the interviewer will be primarily seeking the answers to the questions shown in Exhibit 3.2. However, it is not wise to have such a chart in front of him and to go down the list and check off the answers. This is not designed to deceive the person being interviewed but to keep the interview conversational and informal and to prevent the supervisor from feeling that he or she is being rated as an individual, which is certainly not the intent.

SUPERVISOR'S INTERVIEW SUMMARY

	YES	NO
DOES HE KNOW HOW MANY PEOPLE ARE IN THE DEPARTMENT?	*	
DOES HE KNOW HOW MANY PEOPLE ARE ACTUALLY AT WORK ON THE DAY INTERVIEWED?	*	
COULD HE LOCATE EACH PERSON IN HIS DEPARTMENT?	*	
DID HE KNOW EACH PERSONS SPECIFIC ASSIGNMENT?		
DID HE KNOW WHEN EACH PERSONS CURRENT ASSIGNMENT STARTED?		
WOULD BE COMPLETED?		
DID HE HAVE EACH ONE'S NEXT ASSIGNMENT PLANNED?	*	
DID HE HAVE A **DEPARTMENTAL** WORK PLAN?		
DOES HE KNOW IF THE PLAN IS ON SCHEDULE?	*	
DOES HE ASSIGN WORK DIRECTLY TO EACH PERSON OR WORK GROUP?		
DOES HE RELATE EACH PERSON OR GROUP ASSIGNMENT TO A TIME REQUIREMENT?		
DOES HE INFORM THE PERSON OR GROUP OF THE TIME REQUIREMENT?		
DOES HE MAINTAIN ONGOING RECORDS OF		
WORK INPUT	*	
WORK OUTPUT	*	
BACKLOG	*	
PRODUCTIVITY	*	
DOES HE ADJUST THE WORK FORCE TO FLUCTUATING VOLUMES?		
DOES HE FORMALLY DOCUMENT OPERATIONAL PROBLEMS?	*	
DOES HE FOLLOW UP ON WORK ASSIGNMENTS DAILY?		
HOURLY?		

EACH YES ANSWER HAS A POINT VALUE OF 1.

EXCEL. 17-19   **GOOD**   14-16   **FAIR**   10-13   **POOR** under 10

Exhibit 3-2.

In Exhibit 3.2, note that certain questions are marked with an asterisk. When the answers to these questions are positive, the interviewer must follow up and request further data, or, with the supervisor, verify the accuracy of the information. For example:

1. *How many people are at work today?* Get an actual head count, verify that the answer is correct or not, and mark the chart accordingly.
2. *Do you know if your department is on schedule as of now?* Determine what the schedule is and how the actual schedule is measured against the planned schedule. Is there a true means of determining the schedule position, or is the supervisor just making an assumption.
3. *Do you have a method of measuring the productivity of the department?* What is the method? Does it measure output in terms of units per hour? Per day? Get copies of productivity records.

EVALUATING THE RESULTS OF THE INTERVIEWS

With both the manager's and supervisor's interview forms, the evaluation is one of summing up positives and negatives. Each negative answer demonstrates a decided weakness. Each positive answer demonstrates a strength.

It will be found that the majority of supervisors will not have positive answers to many of the questions. For those that do, the examination of the facts will reveal that the answers have no real basis in fact. The reason that this is true is not a reflection on the supervisor but the result of a lack of training and a lack of management tools that might enable the supervisor to properly manage the time of his people and the other resources under his control. Providing such training and tools will be a prime responsibility of the productivity improvement program and will result, ultimately, in substantial cost reduction.

REVIEW OF HISTORICAL RECORDS

The purpose of a review of historical records will primarily be to investigate the consistency, or more likely, the inconsistency of performance. The company may or may not have the information available in the format that this portion of the analysis requires. If it does not, it will be necessary to go to several different sources to get it. Charting this information is the best way to demonstrate the impact of actual practices and to reveal the potential for improvement.

Exhibit 3.3, a typical example of the kind of information that can be developed, relates the hours worked by month in an order-processing department to the number of orders actually processed. It can be readily seen that the hours of work per order processed vary considerably. Recognize that this is historical information. Later we will make another comparison to demonstrate that the historical performance, when compared to the *ability* of the department to perform, shows even greater inconsistency.

On the basis of the information given and a cost of $7.00 per hour, the order-processing labor cost in October was $2448 higher than in August (2690 × .13 × $7.00). This is a considerable cost variance and strongly indicates a cost reduction potential.

HOURS VERSUS PRODUCTION UNITS

The example above used can be developed in various forms. The elements required are simple; units of work produced and the hours required to produce them. In the exhibit, we find a monthly record, and monthly records tend to have a flattening effect. Though they

Month	June	July	Aug.	Sept.	Oct.
Number of Work Days	22	22	21	21	22
Gross Hours-Eight People	1320	1320	1260	1260	1320
Vacation, Absent Hours	150	165	255	90	105
Actual Hours Worked	1170	1155	1005	1170	1215
Orders Processed	3461	2640	3192	2859	2690
Orders per Hour	2.96	2.28	3.17	2.44	2.21
Hours per Order	.34	.44	.32	.41	.45
Variance Low to High	.13 Hours = 40%				

Exhibit 3-3.

reveal a strong variance, this variance will become more dramatic as the time span is shortened.

For example, in the above example, an actual case, the month of June was broken down into 22 working days. On a day-by-day basis, variances as high as 230% became evident.

Regardless of the type of business, most companies keep records of production in an identifiable unit of measure. They also have records of hours worked. What few do is to actually compare the units and hours to determine the consistency or variances in the output. The higher the variances, the more indication of lack of good operational tools to control costs and therefore greater potential for improvement.

IN-PROCESS TIME VERSUS TIME IN PROCESS

Another technique of analysis is to compare in-process time to the time in process. In any company or department within a company, two elements of information are required.

1. How long it takes, from start to finish to produce an item
2. The actual time applied to the item at each stage of production

In a tool manufacturing company that assembles pliers, a production order was entered into the process on a Monday at 7 A.M. for 2000 pair. The order was completed on Thursday at 2 P.M. The *time in process* was 31 working hours.

The assembly steps were as follows:

1. Code stamp one grip with serial number @ 150/minute
2. Match left and right grip @ 100/minute
3. Rivet left and right grip @ 30/minute
4. Test for key slot tension @ 40/minute
5. Package in individual blister pack @ 150/minute

From this, the *in-process time* figures at 3.5 hours, or approximately 10% of the *time in process*. Even allowing another 10% for material movement, 80% of the *time in process* is waiting time.

This is a strong symptom of lack of scheduling coordination and presents opportunities for considerable reduction of in-process inventory.

INCONSISTENCIES AND BOTTLENECKS REVEALED BY SHIPPING AND DELIVERY RECORDS

Analysis of orders shipped, items mailed, and product received in final goods inventory can reveal the inconsistencies in performance and the possibilities of bottlenecks in the operation.

An analysis conducted in the underwriting department of a New England insurance company revealed that a fixed work force completed only 15% of its policies each week on Monday and Tuesday combined. Wednesday's output went up to 25%. Sixty percent of the output occurred on Thursday and Friday. This is strongly symptomatic of a self-paced work force lacking good supervisory control.

In a New Jersey manufacturing company, 12% of the monthly production was shipped on the last day of the month with a certain degree of regularity. It was determined that the production superintendent substituted an end-of-the-month push for good daily control and was playing catch-up to try to make the month's dollar shipments look good.

These situations reveal weaknesses in the operation and opportunities for improvement.

STANDARD VERSUS ACTUAL PERFORMANCE RECORDS

In any organization that works with engineered time standards, records are available to show actual performance against the standard. These reports normally will reveal worker productivity on a weekly basis or actual versus standard performance on each job completed or some combination of the two. Careful analysis is required, particularly when performance is rated close to 100% and the reports create the impression that everything is close to or on schedule.

One eastern manufacturer produces a daily computer printout by department, by operation, for each process step completed. Performance consistently runs high. An analysis of the actual hours worked in the various departments revealed that only 60% of the time was being recorded against measured work. The other 40% was not productively accounted for. Further analysis demonstrated that the workers were able to leave the department at will when performing unmeasured work, keeping their own pace when working, and, in essence, losing up to half of their production capacity on 40% of the work. Considerable potential for productivity improvement was available.

OBSERVATIONS AS THE KEY TO ANALYSIS

Interviews with management and supervision and looking for variances and problems within company records are usually very revealing and will alert the analyst to the degree of improvement potential from a probability standpoint. Actual observations of the people at work are even more revealing. This portion of the chapter will explain the types of observations that should be made, how to make them, and how to chart results.

NEAR–FAR OBSERVATIONS

The near–far observation is perhaps the simplest one to make and can be done in several different ways. It can be applied to a variety of work activities. Basically it involves observing a worker or workers performing their normal activities at close range with full knowledge on their part that they are being observed. Count the result of their effort. The observation time can be relatively short, say 15 minutes to a half hour.

Move away from the work station to a point where the worker believes that he or she is no longer being observed and continue the observation. Again, count the number of "pieces" produced. For simplicity, use the same length of time for the *far* observation.

Convert both observations into pieces per hour. The results will often be very startling. Exhibit 3.4 is an actual situation from an invoicing department in a lumber sales company.

Another method of the same theme would be to take several *near* observations of the same activity at different times, even on different days. There will probably be slight variances in units per hour from one observation to the other. Then secure the actual production and the actual time spent by the person observed on that particular activity, for a complete day or week. Again, the contrast will be quite startling. Exhibit 3.5, a typical result, is an actual study from an assembly department in an electronic manufacturing company.

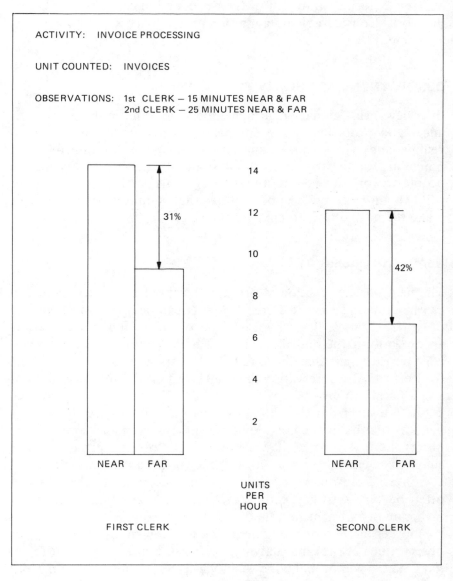

Exhibit 3–4.

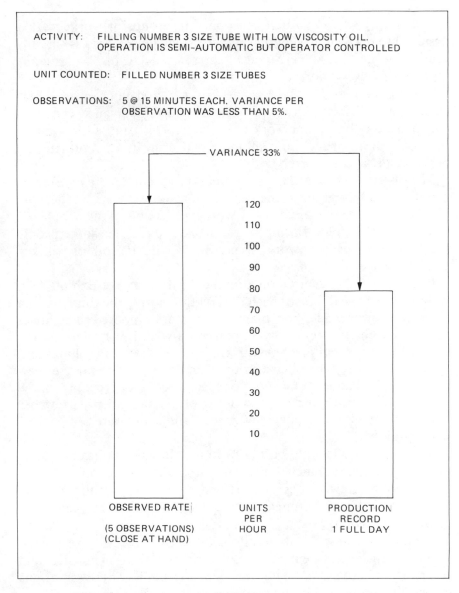

ACTIVITY: FILLING NUMBER 3 SIZE TUBE WITH LOW VISCOSITY OIL.
              OPERATION IS SEMI-AUTOMATIC BUT OPERATOR CONTROLLED

UNIT COUNTED: FILLED NUMBER 3 SIZE TUBES

OBSERVATIONS: 5 @ 15 MINUTES EACH. VARIANCE PER
                OBSERVATION WAS LESS THAN 5%.

VARIANCE 33%

120
110
100
90
80
70
60
50
40
30
20
10

OBSERVED RATE   UNITS   PRODUCTION
                   PER   RECORD
(5 OBSERVATIONS)   HOUR   1 FULL DAY
(CLOSE AT HAND)

Exhibit 3-5.

RATIO DELAY STUDIES

A ratio delay study can best be applied to groups of workers. It is designed to determine what percentage of the time at work is actually productive and what percentage represents delay or lost time. A number of observations are required.

The observer records the date, department, and name of the supervisor on a worksheet. The observer must know, in advance, the number of people that are at work in the area. This can be the number of people in an office, on a shipping platform, in a manufacturing department, and so forth.

The observer goes into the area and quickly counts the number of people actually present in the department, noting as he or she does so, how many people are actively working and how many people are not. It's like taking a flash picture, quick and simple. Some people will be found busily at work, some will be idle, and others will not be in evidence.

Record each observation on a ratio delay format (see Exhibit 3.6). A line will be filled out for each observation noting the time that the observation was made, how many people were supposed to be in the department (crew size), how many were observed working, and the number that were idle. These are recorded under W (working) and I (idle). The difference between the sum of W and I and the crew size is recorded under A (away). For each observation, then, we know that out of a group of a given number of people, a certain number were actually working, others were idle, and some were not at their work stations.

It is important to note on the form the shift (if applicable), start time, break times, lunch times, and stop time. Any observations taken within five minutes of start and stop times or during break periods should be discounted because of the normal delays and inaccuracies that could exist.

Exhibit 3.6 shows 21 observations taken in the inquiry section of a purchasing department. Each column has been downfooted and summarized in the *total* box, lower right. A sampling of observations has been summarized by highlighting them on the form with checkmarks and totalling them in the sample box.

Exhibit 3.7 is a chart based on the sample. It clearly depicts that *lost* time and *away* time in the department amount to a heavy per-

RATIO DELAY

DATE _____

DEPARTMENT_____

SUPERVISOR_____

TIME	CREW	W	I	A	TIME	CREW	W	I	A	TIME	CREW	W	I	A
TUES 11 *AM*	6	4	1	1						*THURS* 9 $\frac{35}{AM}$	8	7	0 -	1
11 ^{07}	6	4	1	1				✓		10 ^{40}	8	5	1	2
11 ^{25}	6	4	2	0	✓					1 $^{25}_{PM}$	8	6	2	0
11 ^{40}	6	5	1	0						1 ^{55}	8	6	2	0
2 ^{10}	8	4	1	3	✓			✓		2 ^{25}	8	2	6	0
2 ^{05}	8	3	2	3	✓			✓		3 ^{10}	8	5	0	3
3 ^{25}	8	5	2	1										
WED. 6 $\frac{30}{AM}$	4	2	0	2	✓									
6 ^{31}	4	2	2	0	✓									
6 ^{37}	4	3	0	1	✓									
6 ^{45}	5	4	1	0										
6 ^{55}	5	5	0	0										
7 ^{40}	8	6	0	2										
7 ^{50}	8	5	2	1	✓									
8 ^{05}	8	7	1	0										
TOTAL	94	63	16	15	TOTAL					TOTAL	48	31	11	6

SHIFT___*ALL*___ NAMES_____

START__6:30 *AM* 4_____
6:45 *AM* 1
7:00 *AM* 2
7:30 *AM* 1

BREAKS____—____

LUNCH __*STAGGERED 1 HOUR*__
11-1

STOP __3:30-4 4:00 2__
3:45-1 4:30 1

ACTIVITY _*RECEIVING AND PROCESSING INQUIRIES*_

TOTAL

W	I	A
(58%)	(29%)	(13%)
94	47	21

SAMPLE(✓)

W	I	A
(53%)	(24%)	(23%)
35	16	15

Exhibit 3-6.

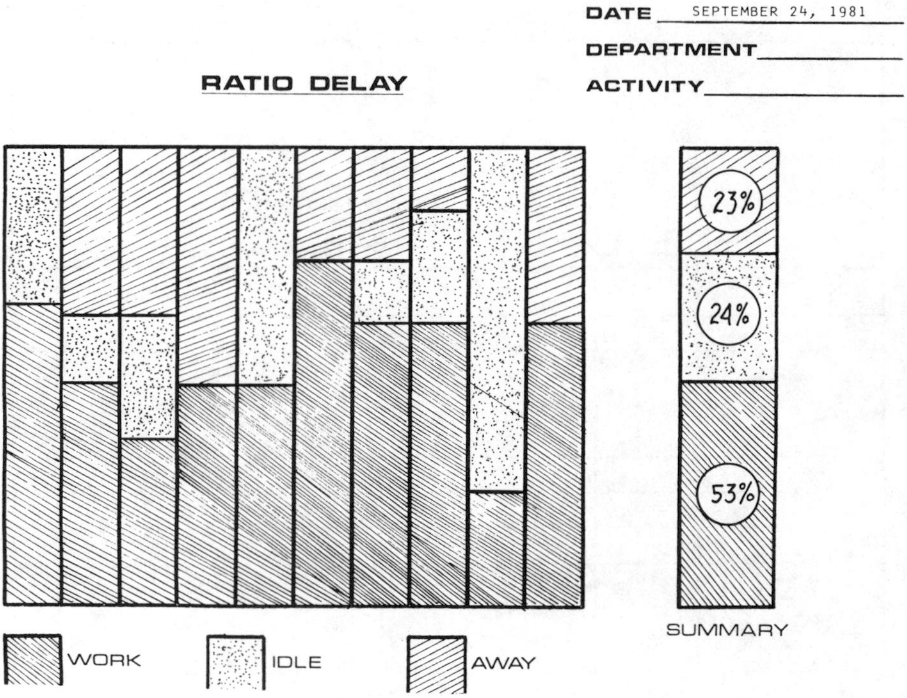

DATE ___SEPTEMBER 24, 1981___

DEPARTMENT_____

RATIO DELAY

ACTIVITY_____

WORK   IDLE   AWAY

SUMMARY

Exhibit 3-7.

centage of available work time. It is rare that the observer will find *less than* 20% outright lost time. Very often it will exceed 30%.

TIME DIARIES

A time diary is the result of a continuing observation of a person or group of people for a specified period of time. Observations of 20 minutes to several hours in duration can be made. The observer must be in a position to distinguish actual work being done from idle time that exists. The record is kept in blocks of time distinguishing between the two. The observations can then be charted as observed and can be charted in summary.

These observations are usually very revealing and reflect direct lost time, much of which can be captured and put back to work.

Exhibits 3.8 and 3.9 are examples of actual diaries that contain lost-time elements that will be found in most instances.

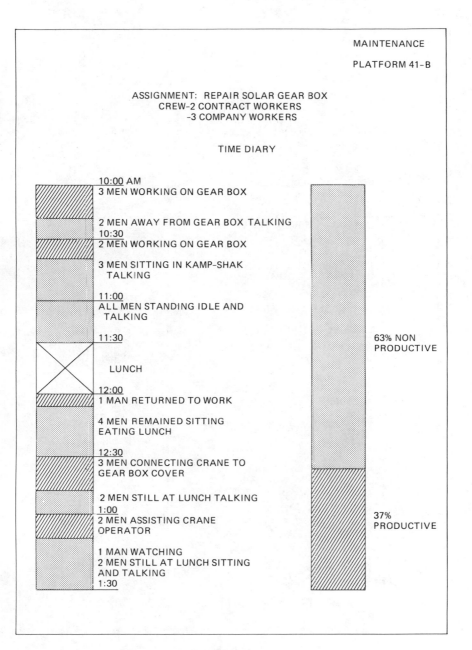

MAINTENANCE

PLATFORM 41–B

ASSIGNMENT: REPAIR SOLAR GEAR BOX
CREW–2 CONTRACT WORKERS
–3 COMPANY WORKERS

TIME DIARY

10:00 AM
3 MEN WORKING ON GEAR BOX

2 MEN AWAY FROM GEAR BOX TALKING
10:30
2 MEN WORKING ON GEAR BOX

3 MEN SITTING IN KAMP-SHAK
 TALKING

11:00
ALL MEN STANDING IDLE AND
 TALKING

11:30

 LUNCH

12:00
1 MAN RETURNED TO WORK

4 MEN REMAINED SITTING
EATING LUNCH

12:30
3 MEN CONNECTING CRANE TO
GEAR BOX COVER

 2 MEN STILL AT LUNCH TALKING
1:00
2 MEN ASSISTING CRANE
OPERATOR

1 MAN WATCHING
2 MEN STILL AT LUNCH SITTING
AND TALKING
1:30

63% NON
PRODUCTIVE

37%
PRODUCTIVE

Exhibit 3–8.

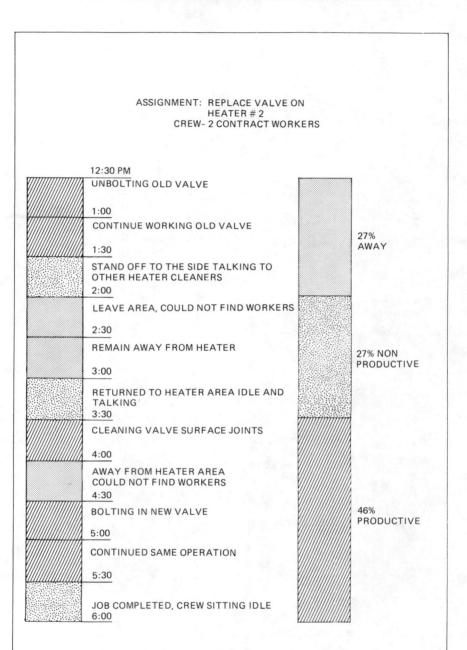

ASSIGNMENT: REPLACE VALVE ON
HEATER # 2
CREW- 2 CONTRACT WORKERS

12:30 PM
UNBOLTING OLD VALVE

1:00
CONTINUE WORKING OLD VALVE

1:30
STAND OFF TO THE SIDE TALKING TO
OTHER HEATER CLEANERS
2:00
LEAVE AREA, COULD NOT FIND WORKERS

2:30
REMAIN AWAY FROM HEATER

3:00
RETURNED TO HEATER AREA IDLE AND
TALKING
3:30
CLEANING VALVE SURFACE JOINTS

4:00
AWAY FROM HEATER AREA
COULD NOT FIND WORKERS
4:30
BOLTING IN NEW VALVE

5:00
CONTINUED SAME OPERATION

5:30
JOB COMPLETED, CREW SITTING IDLE
6:00

27%
AWAY

27% NON
PRODUCTIVE

46%
PRODUCTIVE

Exhibit 3-9.

PERFORMANCE VERSUS ABILITY TO PERFORM

In Exhibit 3.3, we saw a measurement of performance based on actual work output and hours worked. The five month summary showed a total of 14,842 orders processed using 5715 hours or 2.6 hours per order.

Observations were taken on several different occasions that showed an ability on the part of the department to produce at a rate of 3.5 orders per hour. From the number of hours worked for that entire period, it can be determined that the department functioned at only 74% of its capacity.

$$14,842 \div (5715 \times 3.5)$$

The best performance was in the month of August when production reached 91% of capacity

$$3192 \div (1005 \times 3.5)$$

and the worst was the month of October with a performance of 63%.

This type of performance is not unusual. Though it may take considerable time and effort to research and make the observations, the results, most often, will be quite startling. This type of analysis can be applied to any operation where a defined unit for measuring productive output is available.

CALCULATING THE DOLLAR IMPROVEMENT POTENTIAL

In order to determine the priority of a department's position in the program, the real potential for dollar improvement should be determined. Recognize that, at this point, it is not necessary to determine *how* this improvement will be brought about. That will be determined in the actual program development.

Once the analysis reveals that enough symptoms exist to indicate a strong potential for improvement, the degree of that potential can be figured out and a goal established. Exhibit 3.10 shows a 53.6% lost-time factor for a crew of 27 people with an annual wage of $16,250 each. It has been determined that 46.4% of their time is productive and has a value of $203,580. The remaining 53.6% rep-

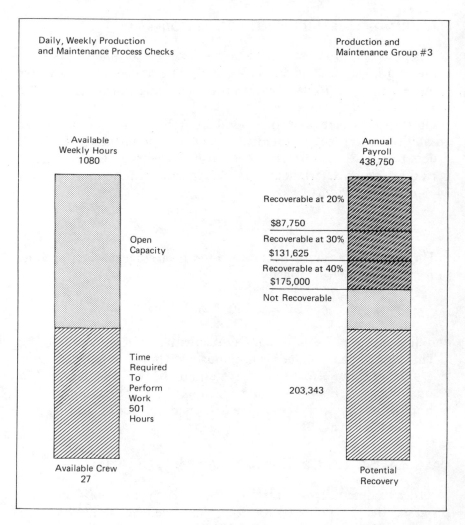

Daily, Weekly Production
and Maintenance Process Checks

Production and
Maintenance Group #3

Available
Weekly Hours
1080

Annual
Payroll
438,750

Open
Capacity

Recoverable at 20%
$87,750

Recoverable at 30%
$131,625

Recoverable at 40%
$175,000

Not Recoverable

Time
Required
To
Perform
Work
501
Hours

203,343

Available Crew
27

Potential
Recovery

Exhibit 3–10.

resents lost time of $235,170. Consideration has been given that 25% of the lost time is most likely not recoverable. This gives a recoverable factor of $175,500 representing 40% of the total payroll.

Targets can be set lower than the 40% and a judicious application of common sense may dictate that a target of 20 or 30% would be more practical and achievable. It is better to set a lower target and achieve more than to set one too high and fall short. During the application of the program, the objective will be to achieve the highest practical figure.

In assuring that all departments receive their proper priority, the recovery percentage should be uniform throughout. The target, though established on the basis of the payroll, does not necessarily mean that payroll will be reduced by the target amount. It means that the cost of doing business in a given department will be reduced when measured against the department output. This could mean an increase in production, reduction of rework, better quality, or any combination of measurable factors. The payroll approach is usually the simplest to apply in arriving at a potential and is normally quite accurate regardless of the way the final results are measured.

PREPARATION OF A PRESENTATION PACKAGE

The person who is given the responsibility for the program can now put together a presentation package for management. This package should consist of charts, as illustrated in this chapter, demonstrating the findings and conclusions. The sum of the potential improvement becomes the key factor for management's determination of how much, in the way of resources, it will commit to the development and implementation of the program and at what speed it wants to progress.

The charts should be well prepared for presentation. Colored charts can be most effective. The presentation should be carefully outlined and clearly demonstrate that the potential exists in fact, not just in theory. The presenter should suggest more than one alternative in terms of the time requirements, manpower needs and other costs.

The presentation should be dramatic and be designed to excite a great deal of interest on the part of top management. It is necessary to create a high degree of enthusiasm for the recovery of the dollar potential. This can be achieved if the presenter has become totally convinced that improvements can be made and that the only requirement left is to work at getting them.

4

Key Elements of a Good Program

The cost reduction/profit improvement program should start off with a *plan* or *schedule*. In each area of application, a means of *measuring results* must be determined. *Progress meetings* involving top management become an integral part of the program. Enlisting the *cooperation* of all personnel is essential. Continuous *follow-up* on a permanent basis and *recording of results* are necessary. This chapter will be about these key elements and how to ensure their necessary integration into the program.

PROGRAM PLAN OR SCHEDULE

Laying out a schedule or plan requires setting realistic goals to achieve full implementation. The program is developed in five basic phases: introduction, detailed analysis, design, implementation, and transition. These phases are laid out on a calendar chart and serve as a track to run on. During the course of the program, it may become necessary to adjust the schedule for many reasons, so it is essential that everyone understand that it is not cut in stone. To ensure that interest is maintained, the schedule should be as short as is practical but long enough to provide ample time for the work that must be done. Sufficient resources should be applied to prevent the program development from stretching out too long.

Introductory Phase

The introductory phase is conducted in *all* departments at the onset. It consists of having the coordinator and those who will actively work on the program with the coordinator get acquainted with the departments with which they will work. Each will spend time with the managers and supervisors of the designated departments. A period of time of two to three days to as much as a week, depending upon the complexity of the department(s), will be planned.

Exhibit 4.1, which shows the beginning of the program schedule, lays out a weekly plan for the introductory phase. It assumes that the coordinator and two others have been assigned to the program and that there are two direct labor departments, a maintenance department, a combined shipping/receiving department, a custodial services department, and a clerical work force.

Each assigned person has a twofold responsibility: to become generally acquainted with the workings of the department and its subsections and to introduce the manager and each of his supervisors to the program goals and their mutual roles in achieving the goals. He will take the opportunity to establish a good working relationship with the manager and supervisors. The entire approach is one of giving assistance to the department in achieving the established goals.

Detailed Analysis Phase

This is, in most instances, the longest phase in the program. The person assigned must become intimately knowledgeable in the workings of the department. Complete knowledge of work flows from beginning to end must be achieved. Volume information on input and output must be obtained. Material flaws as well as all paperwork controls are to be documented. Methods of work assignment should be thoroughly understood along with any required deadlines.

During this phase the relationship between the work to be done and the time it takes to do it is established. In those operations for which time standards already exist, such standards can be used. In others, observations must be made to relate the length of time it takes to perform a unit of work. In still others, particularly in nonrepetitive type of activities, such as maintenance, supervisory estimates can be made. In machine-controlled operations, machine capacities and limitations must be understood. In establishing the schedule for the detailed analysis phase, sufficient time must be allowed to permit the person assigned to accomplish all that is required. This can be quite difficult because of the complex variables

HERIC MANUFACTURING SPECIALTIES

PROFIT IMPROVEMENT PROGRAM

PRELIMINARY SCHEDULE

Department and Assignment	SCHEDULED PHASES BY WEEK NUMBER																						
	1	2	3	4	5	6	7	8	9	10	11	12	13	14	15	16	17	18	19	20	21	22	23
MACHINE AND SHEET METAL Assigned to: Jerry	A																						
ASSEMBLY DEPARTMENT Assigned to: Jerry		A																					
MAINTENANCE DEPARTMENT Assigned to: Bob	A																						
SHIPPING AND RECEIVING DEPTS Assigned to: Bob		A																					
CUSTODIAL SERVICES Assigned to: Morin	A																						
ORDER ENTRY AND ACCOUNTING Assigned to: Morin		A																					

A: INTRODUCTORY PHASE
B: DETAILED ANALYSIS

C: DESIGN PHASE
D: IMPLEMENTATION

E: TRANSITION

Exhibit 4–1.

involved. In a manufacturing operation, for example, it could be relatively simple to absorb all of the details when the various operations are all controlled by means of production-sequenced travelers accompanying each job input. On the other hand, in a clerical operation, it may be necesary to study each position as a separate entity. Details of how this is accomplished are contained in later chapters. Understanding these details enhances the ability to schedule this portion of the program.

By checking Exhibit 4.2, it can be ascertained that the calendar time for this part of the program varies considerably. It is based on a particular sequence in a medium-sized manufacturing firm. Note that the sequence ensures that each of the assigned people are involved in only one department at a time until well into the transition phase.

Design Phase

The design phase is the time when, with the cooperation of the department manager and supervisor, the determination is made as to *how* the resources will be better controlled. The coordinator and/or person assigned will introduce ideas as well as solicit ideas to develop the *tools* that will enable management and supervision to gain complete control over the department. Physical changes that may be required are worked out at this time. Very often, paperwork adjustments have to be made.

In one manufacturing company, a complete relocation of finished goods in the warehouse was necessary to provide proper staging of product for shipping. In another, equipment and machinery had to be moved to allow for the necessary reassignment of personnel. Relocation of desks and even departments in a clerical function is not uncommon when the true work-flow relationships are laid out. In the majority of instances, however, minor adjustments only are required.

The method of control that enables supervisors to recognize those occurrences that interfere with the normal put-through of work should be developed with *early recognition* followed by immediate corrective action as the byword. The designed program is reviewed at all levels, the necessary physical changes made, and the department prepared for implementation.

PRELIMINARY SCHEDULE

SCHEDULED PHASES BY WEEK NUMBER

Department and Assignment	1	2	3	4	5	6	7	8	9	10	11	12	13	14	15	16	17	18	19	20	21	22	23
MACHINE AND SHEET METAL — Assigned to: Jerry	A	B	B	B	B	B	B					C	C	C	C	D	D	D	D	E	E		
ASSEMBLY DEPARTMENT — Assigned to: Jerry		A						B	B	B	B			C	C					D	D	D	E
MAINTENANCE DEPARTMENT — Assigned to: Bob	A		B	B	B	B						C	C				D	D	D	E	E		
SHIPPING AND RECEIVING DEPTS — Assigned to: Bob		A					B	B	B	B	B			C	C			D	D	D	D		E
CUSTODIAL SERVICES — Assigned to: Morin	A		B	B	B									C	C	C		D	D	D	E	E	
ORDER ENTRY AND ACCOUNTING — Assigned to: Morin		A				B	B	B	B	B	B	B				C	C			D	D	D	E

A: INTRODUCTORY PHASE
B: DETAILED ANALYSIS
C: DESIGN PHASE
D: IMPLEMENTATION
E: TRANSITION

Exhibit 4-2.

Implementation Phase

The implementation phase can be divided into two subphases, namely, dry run and actual implementation.

The dry run is, in effect, an exercise designed to test the controls, monitor the changes, and observe possible disadvantages without having an effect on the actual workings of the department. The coordinator, or person assigned, will in effect use the controls on a mock basis while the supervisor assigns his work and runs the department as before. The two then confer, comparing what actually transpired to what could have transpired. The dry run may also take the form of testing the controls or of changes in a small segment of the department.

In a manufacturing company that makes throw-away razors, the process of inserting the blade into the plastic head, and then boxing the head into a package of 5 bladed units, takes place on 2 machines placed across the aisle from each other and controlled and fed by 1 operator. The studies made over a 4 week analysis period showed that the time of the operator was only utilized 15%. It was determined that with a minor modification, an operator could handle 4 machines on either side of the aisle. Since there were 5 lines of 20 machines each, the labor savings could be dramatic. The dry run was accomplished by selecting only 8 machines to be run by 2 operators, neither of whom would cross the aisle and each of whom would handle 4 machines. All went well during the first hour but in the second hour, the 2 operators began to wear down and started missing their load points by a matter of seconds, resulting in gaps in the placing of bladed heads in the boxes. The number of machines was reduced to 3 and the operation went without a flaw. Gradually, the entire department was converted to a 1-on-3, rather than a 1-on-2 operation resulting in a one-third reduction in labor.

This example serves to emphasize the importance of dry running before full or actual implementation. In many types of operations, the dry run can be a paperwork exercise.

The actual implementation takes place when the coordinator, the person assigned, the department management and supervision, and members of any department contributing to the change or the development of the control tools are in agreement that it will work and will not cause problems in the department.

On the schedule, sufficient time is allowed for working out any bugs that may occur. The department supervision and management must feel very comfortable that everything is working well, and the coordinator or person assigned must continue to work right along, monitoring developments.

Transition Phase

Once the implementation has taken place, the coordinator or person assigned must gradually withdraw. Having spent 100% of his time with the supervisor(s) and manager of the department during the initial stages of implementation, he now reduces time spent, perhaps checking at the beginning of the shift to assure that everything starts out well, checking back at the end for a while, and then gradually reducing further. In the meantime the coordinator or assigned person goes on to work at the detailed analytical phase of the next department. Exhibit 4.2 demonstrates the overlap between the transition phase of one area and the detailed analytical phase of another.

It must be recognized that some people will learn faster than others, and, when necessary, the implementation and transition phases may have to be extended. It is better to extend them than sacrifice complete and thorough indoctrination and compliance.

MEASURING RESULTS

In any application of cost reduction/profit improvement techniques, success can only be realized when the results of the effort can be adequately measured in terms of real dollars. It is very important that a method of taking this measurement be developed for each area. Some will be simple and very direct. Others will be more difficult and require considerable effort to develop.

Same Amount of Work at Less Cost

In any department that has production restrictions because of limited input or capacity, history shows us that certain cost factors are present. Most likely, labor costs, in terms of hours worked, are the same in the short run. Material costs show some fluctuations because of scrap variances but over a period of time are relatively stable. In a clerical operation, the numbers of people, historically, remain steady.

The effort, in such situations, should be aimed at reducing costs for the same amount of work. The establishment of control at the supervisory level will result in a reduction of the work and faster put-through of paperwork. Each of these factors can readily be measured.

In the example of the blade manufacturer, the reduction in labor hours per unit of production was quite obvious. Actually, a second benefit accrued. With the attention time of the people increased from 15 to 45%, less time was available for idleness, and the workers' attentiveness resulted in decreased downtime. The ultimate result was an increase in *good* product as well as the labor reduction. Both factors contributed to the same measurement; a reduced labor hour cost per unit of production. In the order-processing department of a large New York manufacturing concern, the program resulted in a reduction of 22% of the work force. Such a reduction was directly measured by a decrease in payroll dollars.

More Output with the Same Resources

In instances where more work has always been available than the department could produce, the program will result in increased productivity. When productivity records are maintained, the percentage increase will become obvious and a dollar figure can be calculated per point of increase.

In many types of operations, historical data is usually available in terms of some kind of number. For example, in a large hospital in New England, the program as applied to the ward clerks was measured by the number of hours of clerical time per patient day. These hours were considerably reduced as the result of the program, and as the patient census increased or decreased, the hours could be adjusted accordingly.

Reduction of In-Process Inventory

In-process inventory is a more difficult unit to measure and may not be immediately available. Many manufacturing companies only take inventory of in-process material on an annual basis for tax purposes.

This is a long-range measurement. Better planning and control, however, will normally result in a decrease of the time in process. Inventory taking will reveal that the amount of material and labor stored in the flow can be considerably reduced. A midwest manufacturer of electronic components determined that *in-process inventory* values had been reduced more than three quarters of a million dollars, a 17% improvement.

Variable Volume Situations

In any department or area in which seasonal or other volume fluctuations usually occur, the measurement of results must normally be applied to a given unit of production, involving, of course, a determination of what that unit should be. Often this is straightforward, as in the experience of a bottler of fine whiskey in Kentucky whose volume fluctuated greatly. The unit was the bottle or, to be more exact, cases of bottles coming off the line. The labor and machine hours to produce a given number of bottles or a case was readily measured.

However, in a machine shop producing a large variety of parts, the answer may not be as simple. If productivity measurements exist, improvement may show up in this record. Attention should be turned to the productive hours spent on measured work. A twofold measurement of increased productivity as well as increased hours of productive work may well be the answer.

Basically, the means to measure results can be found in most companies' historical records. When such records, on rare occasions, do not exist, it may be necessary to establish a reporting system at the outset of the detailed analysis phase and run the record for the duration of that phase. Comparison with this record can be made following implementation.

Progress Meetings

Recognizing that the ultimate responsibility for the success of the program rests with top management, those directly involved, and in particular, the coordinator, have a responsibility to apprise the upper echelon of the progress of the program up to and including the complete implementation of all phases in all departments. These progress meetings should have meaning and substance. Meetings that are dry and boring should be avoided at all costs. Sufficient time should be allowed to cover the essentials. A written agenda must be prepared. If management decisions are to be requested, this information should be transmitted in advance to all those involved in the decision-making process.

Frequency of Meetings

In most programs, meetings should be scheduled a minimum of once a month. Less frequent meetings could result in a diminution of interest. More frequent meetings are desirable when the program is fast paced and when results begin to accumulate. The frequency will also be governed by the availability of the people that should attend. It is best to establish specific dates at the outset, and if possible, the same day of the week and time of day should be used to enable key people to plan their calendars. Require, out of courtesy, that any person not able to attend, notify the others.

The Need for Substantive Meetings

The key to a good meeting is to present something of substance. A dramatic result with its attending benefits will capture the attention of everyone. Presentation of an *opportunity* for benefits can also pique the interest of the group. This is particularly true when potential improvement can be demonstrated and the management group is presented with having to make a decision to achieve these benefits. If the decision is not to be made at that time, a deadline for the decision can be established.

Requests for action and for participation of members of the management team should be presented at the meetings. These can be very specific such as requesting the vice president of personnel to look into the reasons for a recalcitrant supervisor or manager's lack of interest or cooperation. If support assistance is needed, the meeting is the place to request it.

The progress meeting is also a format for checking the status of the program's development. The events that have taken place since the previous meeting are announced, and the plans for the next several weeks should be reviewed.

Before the meeting ends, the date for the next meeting should be confirmed. The coordinator should follow up with a written confirmation sent to each participant. Prior to the next meeting, the new agenda is to be published.

ENLISTING COOPERATION

To assure full cooperation of all concerned and to maintain continued interest in the program's development, it is necessary to focus attention on the benefits of the program. This does *not* mean that the cost reduction benefits to the company are the paramount items to be emphasized. Such benefits may be topmost in the minds of executives, but as you go down the ladder, you discover the things that motivate people will vary—at each level of management and, within each level, by individual.

Perhaps the most significant motivational tools, those that will help to ensure cooperation and even enthusiastic participation, are involvement, job satisfaction, personal opportunity, and monetary award. Each of these can be made an integral part of the entire effort.

INTRODUCING THE PROGRAM

An announcement by the company to all employees that a program is to be undertaken can get things off to a good start. The media for the announcement will vary by management style and company procedure. The house organ, if one exists, can be used. Notices on bulletin boards can be effective. A series of meetings starting with department heads and working downward can be effective.

The announcement must focus on the benefits that each individual can derive. It must also emphasize the opportunity for contribution on the part of all concerned. There is no secret formula to accomplish this. It will be as varied as the personality of the firm. The approach must always be in a positive vein.

In one large company, which was hiring a team of consultants to work on the development of the program, a notice was placed on the bulletin board that simply stated that a program of improving performance was being initiated. It congratulated all employees and supervisors on their past performance and emphasized that the program would be a learning experience for all of them and would benefit all.

A New York bank chose to have a series of meetings. The top management met with the middle management group, emphasizing that their full participation and cooperation was essential to success and that their opportunities would be enhanced by that success. They in turn were to hold meetings with their managers and so on down the line, with the emphasis being altered to appeal to each level. The key at the supervisory level was job enrichment and monetary rewards.

With the work force, the supervisor of each area should emphasize the need for cooperation and participation through the premise that improved performance will mean greater job satisfaction, improved conditions of work flow, as well as a means of pinpointing problems that interfere with the ability to keep the jobs running smoothly. He or she can also emphasize that the program opens a new door for the workers in communicating their ideas upward through the "Action Needed" part of the program (Chapter 6).

FOLLOW-UP AND RECORDING

Every program requires a means of follow-up and a continuing recording of results. The need is best met by a reporting system that is built into the program in a pyramiding fashion so that it originates at the lowest supervisory level and moves upward.

Chapter 11 goes into the details of reporting and follow-up. In developing the method of *recording* data, simplicity must be the key. In many companies, the communication network already contains the system, and all that is required are minor changes to relate the data to the program function.

Exception Reporting

Exception reporting is a key to the follow-up procedure. It starts with the early recognition by the supervisor that something has gone off schedule. He reports the fact or problem and what corrective action he took immediately to solve it. When the problem is beyond his control, he reports it upward for corrective action at the next level of management. The program will require that he not only record the fact and report it but that he be able actually to demonstrate the seriousness of the loss.

It is not unusual to find foremen and supervisors responding to this procedure in a very positive fashion. Too often, they receive a report in the middle of *this* week that *last* week's results were poor. All of the data that were generated through the system have to be fed into the computer by week's end, and several days go by before the results are generated and distributed. By the time the supervisor receives last week's results, he is half way through the current week and many of the problems that existed then continue to exist, but have not been recognized. Under the program, the means will be established to give immediate recognition to problems, lead to their early solution, and improve results. Instead of his *being told* that performance was down in an after-the-fact report, the foreman or supervisor will be *telling* up front that a problem occurred, caused a specific loss, and was corrected early on.

Measuring Results against a Base

Part and parcel of follow-up and recording is the establishment of a base against which results can be measured. As described earlier in this chapter, this base is the performance that history reveals. In the follow-up and recording process, measuring improvements against the base enables all contributors to receive recognition. After a time, the base can be moved to a new level of performance, adding a challenge to seek additional ways of improving.

A large national hotel chain, after having its program in place for a full year, realized a two million dollar and more improvement on the bottom line while holding down its rates of increase. In the second year, having moved its base forward, an additional million dollars was added to the profit picture through innovative improvements. The challenge was made via the recording procedure and the resulting follow-up by the coordinator's staff.

In developing the program, those responsible should be aware of the basic elements outlined here. Their application will give credence to the program and go a long way to contributing to its ultimate success.

5

Supervisory Training for Cost Reduction/Profit Improvement

Cost reduction cannot take place effectively in the corporate board-room or the president's office. At these levels of decision, a program to achieve results can be formulated and the wheels put in motion. The point of execution is at the level of the first-line supervisor. It is only through his day-to-day effort that the company's resources are properly brought together and utilized to gain maximum results. Yet, he is often the least trained in the necessary techniques and has not been provided with the required tools of control. The first-line supervisors interview as illustrated in Chapter 3 will reveal this fact very clearly.

A very important part of the program, supervisory training must take place. A good portion of it will occur as the program develops in each supervisor's area. Additionally, though, he must be taught just what the job of supervisor consists of: how work can be planned, organized, and controlled. He must know how to communicate his expectations to his people and motivate them to respond. He must know how to assign work, follow up on the assignments, and evaluate results. Throughout the program, the supervisor must be taught the theory, and more important, the application of these principles.

THE SUPERVISOR'S JOB

The supervisor is the person in the middle between management and the work force. The workers will interpret management's goals and attitudes through the supervisor. How effectively he demonstrates these to the workers depends on how well his own goals and attitudes are in tune with management's. So first of all, he must be oriented to the management of the company.

He must be objective in dealing with people and situations, giving recognition when due. Judging ideas by their merit, listening willingly and with an open mind, readiness to praise as well as criticize, and willingness to enforce company rules even-handedly, are all necessary elements of the job.

His job involves the planning of the work to be done. This includes knowing what work is available or will become available, what tools, equipment or machinery will be needed to accomplish the work, and assuring that they are on hand. He must match the availability of labor hours to the workload. In accomplishing this, he must be aware of his priorities and plan the work accordingly.

The supervisor's job, in most instances, will consist of assigning the work to his people, or in some cases, being aware of each worker's load and having a method of knowing the progress of the work. Following up on assignments to ensure the timely accomplishment of work involves knowledge of the relationship of the work to the time required to do it. The supervisor's control must include the tools necessary to alert him to conditions or problems that interfere with the put-through of work. His job consists of taking remedial action to correct such situations.

Training of employees is an important part of the supervisory responsibility. The supervisor must have sufficient knowledge of the workings of his department to ensure that all employees are trained in their specific duties and tasks. This is *not* to imply that an office supervisor must be able to teach typing or that a foreman must be able to teach an operator to run a lathe. It means that he must be able to train people with such knowledge in how their skills will be used in his department.

Reporting results of the department's performance is a requirement that, once understood, ensures that the supervisor is in charge. To properly report results, he must employ all of the techniques of supervision. The results should reflect the plan, how well actual performance went against the plan, what exceptions occurred, and what was done to overcome the exceptions.

To sum up, the supervisor's job consists of managing the resources at his command to achieve the best possible results.

PLANNING AND ORGANIZING FOR CONTROL

The planning function requires knowledge on the part of the supervisor as to:

- *How* much work must be accomplished
- *What* tools and manpower are required
- *When* the work will be started and completed
- *Where* it will go when completed

Training the supervisor in the planning function will involve, at the onset, a determination that the methodology for planning for his department exists. For example, in a machine shop, it is not sufficient for the job card to specify the number of pieces to be produced and the rate of production in terms of minutes per piece. This information provides the basis for an after-the-fact report. The job card should extend the volume and rate into pieces per hour and/or total run time. With this information, the supervisor can be taught to plan the use of the equipment and manpower in terms of time. By establishing elements of time as applied to units of work, the extension by volume provides a meaningful planning tool. The training begins by demonstrating this factor to the supervisor and determining with him, the extent to which his input does or does not contain such elements. When they do not, the next step is to determine how these relationships can be developed. The supervisor may require the assistance of the coordinator or person assigned to the department. This is one of the reasons why the detailed analysis phase of the program can be quite long and involved. Several methods exist to establish the work-time relationship in a meaningful manner.

In those cases in which the work has been measured, and the basic relationship of time to a unit of work has been established, it is only necessary to convert this data by volume into a time for the job or into units per hour. When the material and job card arrive at the department, the necessary planning data is on the card. The card should also be specific in designating the tooling required for each process step and the set-up time required. With this information, the job can be planned in the department's work flow.

When the work-time relationship does not exist, it must be established. In some cases, the resources of the industrial engineering department may be required to make time studies. Because the use of the data for planning and scheduling takes precedence over the after-the-fact measurement of productivity, four decimal accuracy is not essential. The relationship can be established by observation, without a stop watch or by estimate on the part of a knowledgeable person (perhaps the foreman himself). The important aspect of this calculation is that, in the final result, the work must be easily interpreted into meaningful time elements.

Once the time elements are established and the means of interpretation by volume into the time required are provided, the next step is to provide the supervisor with as simple a means of applying these factors to his operation as can be developed. This important aspect of his training will be as varied as the type of work and complexity of the department, but certain principles can be applied.

First, the supervisor must learn to recognize priorities. This can be accomplished by staging, as in the case of a manufacturing department, or through scheduling by production control. Priorities can be set for clerical operations by establishing target times for completion, for maintenance operations by a matrix of priority definitions.

Second, the planning function must match the hours of work to be accomplished to the man and/or machine hours available to accomplish the work, or the exact reverse: The man or machine hours are allocated to accomplish a given amount of work. This latter situation is used when available capacity is greater than the work input.

As a simple illustration, take the case of planning the work for a drilling machine on a given day. The first job assignment is determined to take two and a half hours including the set up. The material and fixturing are made available and moved to the drill machine by start time of 8:00 in the morning. It is now known that the job should be completed by 10:30. The second job in the priority for the day is a four hour run. It is planned that this will start at 10:30 and (allowing for break and lunch) should be completed by 3:15, leaving one and a quarter hours of the workday available for a third job to be planned.

The main thrust in the supervisor's training is to make him aware, provide him the information, and teach him how to use the information to plan his department's activity. This can be accomplished, in theory, through classroom sessions in which the basic requirements are taught in principle. The supervisor is then instructed to apply the principles in theory to his own department. In three to four one-hour weekly sessions between which the supervisor returns to his department and *in theory* works on the planning problem, returning to class with his questions and difficulties, he can be taught to:

- Define work-time relationships
- Convert them by volume into a meaningul plan
- Plan the work of the department

During this period, the coordinator or person assigned to develop the program in the department is working along with him, doing much of the tedious observations and getting agreement from him that the observations are valid. The necessary changes in input data, where applicable, are worked out and made. The actual development of all the data may take longer than the three to four weeks but the basic training will have been accomplished.

ASSIGNING AND CONTROLLING

Once the ability to plan the work in terms of matching time has been accomplished, the method of work assignment is relatively simple. It consists of training the supervisor to ensure that work is always available, the next job is ready for each worker or group of workers, and is provided to them on a timely basis. Normally, the physical makeup of the department and the type of work flow will dictate the method to be used. Later chapters will cover a variety of methods.

The methods of controlling the work must also be specifically designed for each area. However, the theory and reasoning behind the control can be established as a part of general training.

In order to exercise control, the supervisor must know:

- What each person is assigned to do
- When the assignment started
- When the assignment should be completed
- Interim points of checking progress

- How to recognize an "off-schedule" condition
- How to take corrective action

Mastery of these points requires training in the use of the controls that will be developed for the individual department. In order to develop the controls, the supervisor must believe in the theory of control. By having the basic principles implanted in his mind and with the assistance of the person assigned to train him, he will begin to recognize how best to develop the principles of control in his own work environment. Years ago, in the machine shop of an upstate New York manufacturer, unique controls were developed for the foreman that serve to illustrate the point.

The job operation cards were converted to show the setup and the run-time for each operation. A staging area was laid out, and the planning function was well developed. Work assignments were made by having the material and fixturing moved to the equipment prior to the end of the previous job or simultaneously with the removal of the product from the work station. However, there were over 20 machinists and drill press operators to control. An attempt was made to list all the jobs on paper, record the start time, calculate the planned completion time, and establish control. The number of operations per day made this virtually impossible.

The foreman and the coordinator studied the problem for several days and finally hit upon a solution. They had a board built on a stand and on the board provided a "pocket" for each worker in the department and put his name underneath. The pocket would contain the control copy of the job card. Over each pocket, a plastic clock face, with movable hands, was installed.

As each job was assigned, and the card dropped in the pocket, the foreman would check the start time and required time for the operation and move the hands of the clock to the planned stop time. Once the assignments were made and all the clocks set, he could check out the jobs in the order of the shortest clock time, assure that the job was proceeding, take corrective action on a timely basis if problems developed, and get the next assignments ready to move. He had established control. Once the principle was understood, the application followed.

In assigning work, the supervisor must have an expectation of the quality and quantity of work to be accomplished and must communicate it to the worker. For example, it is not enough to send a maintenance man to make a repair. The problem should be defined as accurately as is possible. When applicable, the necessary tools should be made available and, more important, an estimated time of completion should be made. All of this information can be communicated on a maintenance work ticket. If any verbal instructions are needed, they should be precise. When the person goes out on the job, he should have a clear understanding of what is expected of him.

FOLLOW-UP

One of the key weaknesses to be found in most management and supervisory performances is failure to follow up. How can a supervisor, with many things to control, be expected to follow up on all of them?

The key to good follow-up is an ability to recognize *when* to follow up. By establishing plans, the points of follow-up are built in. For example, if the plan calls for certain jobs to be completed at specific times, the obvious point of follow-up is the exception—that job that is not completed on time as specified. The supervisor who is paying attention to his daily plan should have no difficulty in recognizing the time of day as related to his job plan, then following up on the exception.

To provide foremen with an early warning system, one New Jersey manufacturer developed a simple pigeon hole arrangement as a tool for the foremen. There were eight pigeon holes, one for each hour of the day. It was a simple matter for each foreman to insert his control copy in the hour hole designated for the planned completion time. He would remove the copy as jobs were completed so that at the end of any given hour, the copies still in the hole were the exceptions and demanded follow-up. This was a simple tool to train the foremen to use.

Simple Ghant charts can be effective: a time bar across the top with the names of employees down the left. As each assignment is made, a line is drawn to the planned stop time to provide a recognition point. Ghant-type charts are also very good tools to use in classroom training since they can clearly illustrate the principles of logical control points. Exhibit 5.1 is a Ghant chart that illustrates the layout of a daily plan for a variety of situations. The time bar across the

DAILY SCHEDULE   DAY: DATE:

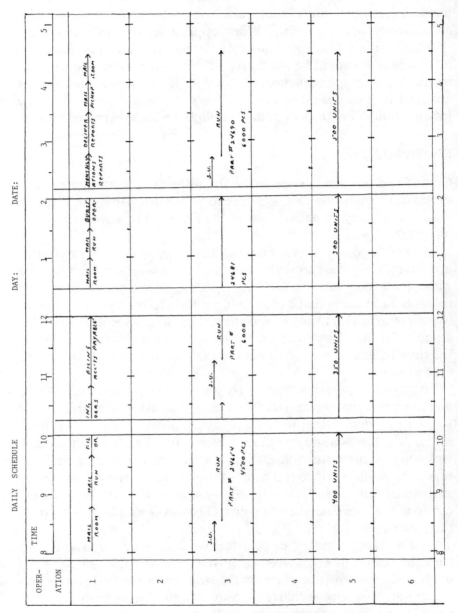

Exhibit 5-1.

horizontal axis represents a full working day with an A.M. break of 15 minutes, a half hour lunch period, and a 10 minute P.M. break.

The illustration on line 1 shows the layout of a daily plan for a clerical-type operation consisting of a variety of different chores, each of which has been interpreted in terms of a time factor. The clerk's work plan for the day has been laid out. Each arrowhead can be used as a checkpoint to determine that the work has been completed up to that point.

The same basic principle has been laid out on line 3, but in this instance we are dealing with a machine setup and run-time for several jobs through the day. The checkpoints are the setup and run arrowheads.

Line 5 shows a job that runs continuously. The checkpoints are those points in time that a certain volume of output can be expected. The volume is shown on a cumulative basis for each arrowhead. The checkpoints are the logical break times during the day.

The exhibit demonstrates that a plan for the day has been made, provides points for the supervisor to check on progress, and brings his attention to the job at sufficiently short intervals to take corrective action if things are not going as planned. It helps put him in control. In the case shown on line 3, it also provides points in time for the supervisor to recognize that he must get the parts and fixturing ready for the next job to avoid delays. All of these insights can be made as principles in the training process, triggering the imagination of the supervisors as to how they can apply them in their own departments.

TRAINING OF EMPLOYEES

In this segment of the chapter, the emphases is on training employees to function as members of the department team, not on the technical aspects of the job. To accomplish this type of training, the supervisor must learn to handle people. He must recognize that each member of his department is an individual with unique characteristics, a person with individual needs, desires, attitudes, and responses. How then, does he motivate them, retain their interest, and make them contributing members of the team? The answers are actually built into his program.

First of all, people want to know what is expected of them. A person assigned a job to do, be it a work order, an area to clean, a clerical task to perform, or just about any type of work, will normally try to meet the expectation of the supervisor. The supervisor must recognize this. Upon making his assignments, he should inform people, in each instance, what he expects from them. They should know *how much* they are expected to produce in a given time period. As the supervisor puts his plan into effect, he communicates to the worker that he expects a certain level of production. The time period of assignment should be of reasonably short duration. By this we mean several hours to a full day in most instances. The supervisor conveys this short-term goal to the employee. The employee reacts to the short-term goal as an immediate challenge to perform. Its like a golf game. A golfer doesn't play to the course par. He plays to the par of each individual hole.

Also, knowing what par is, the supervisor can adjust the attainment of par to an expectation of performance that is in line with the worker's experience and ability. He must recognize that not all persons can perform at par but those that cannot should be aware of par and encouraged to try. He must also learn that the tools of control are not hammers or whips with which to beat on people but rather chisels to help shape them and hoes to cultivate them.

The supervisor must learn to react to his people in a positive way. As he gets more involved with the program, he will become more involved with his people as individuals and as his team. If he conveys the requirements established by the program to them through a positive approach in a positive fashion, they will react in kind.

The supervisor of a stock transfer clerical group in a New England bank with a work force of about 20 people feared that her group would react negatively to the implementation of the program in her area. She recalled, from the training sessions related to employee motivation, that individual recognition of employees was a big factor in getting them to respond. She set up her program as a "target" game. The program production requirements were the targets. Each person was made aware of the target. Her expectation was that everyone would shoot for the target but realistically might not hit it right off and particularly might not hit the bullseye. She constructed a target with four rings. The bullseye was 100, the next ring 90, the third, 80, and the fourth, 70. The "arrows" were arrow- shaped cards with the names of the individuals on them. Each week, she pinned each arrow that got 70% or better to the appropriate ring of the target. Everyone in the department strove to get his or her name on the target. This goal was accomplished in three weeks. She made sure that her department head came around each week to congratulate those people that achieved 90 or 100%. Each person in the department tried to reach that goal.

In the meantime she began to work with the lower achievers to ferret out problems that hindered their production and found a myriad of correctable items that enhanced performance. People began to realize that the supervisor was getting involved with them as individuals and appreciated the attention and recognition. The morale of the department soared. Requests for transfers dropped, and attrition was reduced by 70%. As performance increased, backlogs of work came down and the service level of the department improved. The cost per unit of work went down, and the improvement targeted for the department by the program was exceeded.

This supervisor recognized the need for motivation and acted accordingly. Too often, a supervisor will allow something new to disrupt, confuse, or discourage people. With proper training, they learn to understand what motivates people. The training in the technical aspects of managing their human resources must be accompanied by training in the human relations aspect of their job. The two become an unbeatable combination.

REPORTING RESULTS

How often has a supervisor said, "I'm the last one to know!"? Too often, in most companies. Take the case of the foreman of a component production department in a Maryland manufacturing firm. On a Tuesday afternoon, the production superintendent called him into the office and gave him a tongue lashing about the 10% productivity drop in his department for the prior week. The foreman was astonished. He had been vaguely aware that several problems related to productivity had been present during the week, but a 10% drop was a complete surprise. His boss knew of the problem before he did, as did the boss's boss and the clerk in the mailroom. The foreman would not get his copy of the computer printout until Wednesday morning.

This type of situation has become all too common in our highly computerized society. Production results are fed into computers, measured against standards, accumulated for a specified time period, calculated, printed, and distributed. The foreman or department head is at the tail end of the distribution.

This situation must be reversed. This is not to say that such reporting has no value. It does. However, it must be preceded by a report *from* the foreman or department head that indicates he is aware of his problems as they occur, knows his results as they are achieved, and is not surprised by the final tally that comes out of the computer as an after measurement of performance.

The first-line supervisor must be attuned to his department. To ensure that he is attuned, a simple method of reporting by him, rather than to him, must be devised, and he must be trained in its development and application.

The reporting method should be concise and concerned with the exceptions. It can be as simple as having the foreman or supervisor report only on exceptions—those things that went wrong. This type of reporting must be built into every department in the program, for it is the one sure way to have the foreman recognize problems and handle them.

Using line 3 of Exhibit 5.1, assume that at 8:30 in the morning, checking to see if the setup on the first job was completed, the foreman goes to the machine and finds that the operator has not completed the setup and the run will not start on time, with the result that the entire day's plan will be off schedule almost from the start. He takes the corrective action required—let's say in this case, calling a toolmaker in from the tool room, who solves the problem—but a half hour has been lost. That time is not recoverable but it has been minimized through the early warning system. This triggers him to recognize that Part #24690 will not be run out by the end of the day. He has several choices. He can authorize overtime to complete the run on Part #24690. He can plan to have enough of that part moved to its next operation so that it will not be held up the following day, or he can accept the half hour loss and do nothing.

However, by having to report the "exception" he provides his boss an insight as to his management thinking. The report could be a simple statement of what went wrong, what he did about it, and the result of his action. Such a report would demonstrate that first of all he was paying attention and recognized the problem at an early stage. It would further illustrate that he took appropriate immediate action to minimize the loss. Finally, it would demonstrate his management thinking related to his total schedule and open the door for his boss to evaluate his action and, if required, use the episode for training him in corrective action techniques.

Since episodes of missed schedules are a common occurrence, the experience is repeated continuously. The reporting mechanism places a requirement on the foreman to react. His reactions, then, become the catalyst that furthers his training on a continuing basis.

THE IMPORTANCE OF COMMUNICATIONS

The reporting function is an aspect of the communications that are built into the program. The report opens the door for dialogue between the supervisor and the manager and is a vehicle to improve on-the-job training of the supervisor. Equally important is the necessity of training the supervisors in communication skills to improve their relations with the people under their control.

Clarity in communicating is essential. There is no room for ambiguity. Supervisors must be able to communicate verbally with their employees in such a way that each employee understands, that is, in a clear, concise, informative manner. This type of communication skill can be taught in classroom sessions, through written exercises, and role-playing techniques. The principle of tell, show, and feedback can readily be taught in this manner and through the development of simple exercises.

Communication is a two-way street. Listening and understanding are as important as being able to convey ideas. A supervisor must be a good listener if he is to stimulate a two-way flow of ideas. Failure to listen is counterproductive and gives rise to too many errors and misunderstandings. The responsibility for being a good listener rests more heavily with the supervisor than does the responsibility of being a good communicator with the employee. The supervisor must learn the rules of good listening.

The first rule is to pay attention. Do not allow sights and sounds to distract from the ability to hear and understand. Second, do not hesitate to ask questions and ensure that all of the facts have been brought forth. Finally, assuming that the person communicating is expecting some kind of response, the supervisor must repeat back to that person his understanding of what was communicated.

The supervisor that masters the rules of good communication will not only find that he or she is more persuasive in obtaining the compliance of the workers but will find them more efficient and cooperative.

THE PAPERWORK PROBLEM

Time and time again, when involved with supervisory training programs over the years, the author has encountered supervisors' chronic complaint of too much paperwork and not enough time to do the job of supervising. Very often this is true, and just as often, it is because of the inability of the supervisor to properly organize his time to accomplish the paperwork required. Because the introduction of a productivity improvement program will, in many instances, add some type of paperwork to the supervisor's job, it becomes important to teach him to handle the paperwork of his entire responsibility.

So, as part of the training process, the paperwork entailed by each part of the supervisor's duties must be examined. Each supervisor should be required to produce a sample of each item of paperwork that he is responsible for and the frequency and volume of each. Next, he should be instructed to actually record the time that he spends on each type. For example, if he is currently required to make up a daily time sheet for the department from employee time cards, he should time himself on the actual hours and/or minutes spent making up the time sheet, exclusive of interruptions and distractions. If the total time requirement established for all of the paperwork exceeds 20% of his time, it is cause to examine what the potential is for reducing the burden. However, care must be exercised to differentiate between that paperwork that is of an administrative nature and that which is a distinct part of the function of supervision. If a working supervisor, one whose position requires the processing of certain nonadministrative and nonsupervisory paperwork, is involved, these factors must be considered.

The reduction of administrative paperwork can best put the supervisor in the proper mood for accepting the program. This is not always practical or achievable. However, the supervisor's work habits, as related to the paper can be examined and he can be trained to accomplish it in less time, with fewer distractions. There are points of time during the day that are more suited for paperwork than others. The supervisor can be trained to seek these out, avoiding the worst and using the best.

RECOGNITION OF RESPONSIBILITY

The training of the supervisor, as indicated in this chapter, is based on what his or her job really consists of. The points brought out for emphasis in the training process are fundamental to supervisory performance. Too often, the principle of resource management is not recognized, yet this is why the supervisory position exists. Once this is brought home to the supervisor, his performance will improve. As the program develops in his area, he will more readily accept his part in it. He will recognize that his company is making every effort to provide him with the proper tools to carry out his responsibility.

6

Action-Needed Plan

There is no better way to get *everyone* involved in cost reduction or profit improvement programs than the introduction of a formal plan to get people to think about their jobs and ways to improve them. There is no better way to solve existing problems than to have them brought to the attention of management and, more important, to assure that they get the proper handling in seeking solutions. If nothing else were to be done in the way of a cost reduction/profit improvement program, the *action-needed plan* would still produce results. As an integral part of an overall program, it makes a great contribution.

WHAT THE PLAN IS AND IS NOT

It must be recognized that the plan is not a suggestion program and those companies that have a formal suggestion program must be sure to make the proper distinction.

The *action-needed plan* is a formal means to correct operating problems in order to minimize interruptions and other situations that interfere with the normal function of any department. It is a plan to communicate these problems in an upward direction until the proper level of management has been reached, which can solve the problem and cause corrective action to be taken. The plan requires that the problem be specific in nature. It does *not* require that the person submitting the problem also submit a solution since this may require considerable analysis. This is the major departure from a suggestion program.

BENEFITS OF THE PLAN

Hidden in the work flow of every company are a myriad of problems that, for one reason or another, have become an accepted part of doing business. They are so commonplace that they have been ignored, or even worse, have long been given up on as far as solutions are concerned. The introduction of one basic principle of a good cost reduction program, that of an early recognition that a problem exists, will begin to bring to the surface many of these problems. Some, the supervisor will recognize. Others will be forthcoming from the workers as the supervisor follows up on the schedule exceptions. Many of these problems will be solvable at the supervisor-worker level by immediate or short- range solutions that require no higher authority.

The more difficult problems, however, those requiring the attention of other departments, upper management, technical assistance and so on, form the nucleus of potential cost recovery to which the action-needed approach presents great opportunity. Elimination or reduction of causes of lost time, new approaches to old work-flow interferences, new methods or procedures— all help to increase productivity or directly reduce costs.

The industrial engineering manager of a major New Jersey manufacturer tells the story of how a chronic complaint, long ignored, was funneled through the action-needed plan and ultimately resulted in a $200,000 annual savings. It seems that in one subassembly department, the workers had long complained of problems with broken fingernails and raw fingertips resulting from putting a particular clip on one of the subassemblies that they produced. The problem had been ignored, or more accurately, accepted as a problem, for years. As the result of an action-needed request, the problem *had to be examined* and a formal reply made. It would not be acceptable to just write it off as unsolvable. The problem wound up with a product engineer whose solution was a new clip of a different metal and a simple fixture for attaching it. Not only was the sore finger problem solved but a vast cost reduction was made.

ACTION-NEEDED COMMITTEE

Because the solutions to many problems lie outside the resources or scope of a single area, it is necessary to place problems in the hands of people who can cross departmental lines and whose responsibility it is to resolve the problems. As a matter of fact, people would accept these so-called problems as opportunities, for in the solving of problems is the opportunity for profit improvement.

The action-needed committee will be made up of first-line supervisors from the various departments. This kind of membership will enable them to cross department lines and blend effort, experience, and abilities. The committee would have three permanent members, one of whom would be designated chairperson. The chair could be rotated periodically among the three. The three permanent members should agree to serve for a minimum of a year. At any one time a maximum of two additional temporary members could be introduced to serve when major actions are taken to which they can substantially contribute. In all cases, the members of the committee should be first-line supervisors. No one ranking higher on the chart is to be appointed to the committee.

The chairperson will have the responsibility of calling and conducting meetings, making assignments for problem solving, giving overall direction to the effort, keeping records, and follow-up. Management, for its part, must agree to allow the members of the committee time to hold meetings. A reasonable allotment for this can be arranged. A designated meeting place should be arranged. Necessary file and record-keeping space must be allocated. The committee must be regarded as an integral part of company operations and be given the necessary prestige to enable it to function effectively.

ENCOURAGING FULL PARTICIPATION

All employees, whether supervisory or not, should be encouraged to participate in the action-needed plan. To accomplish this, at its inception, the plan should receive adequate publicity throughout the organization. A write-up in the house organ, if one exists, outlining the plan, its purpose, and goals will be a very good start. Information on the plan posted on employee bulletin boards is another means that can be used. Perhaps the best and most direct way of assuring that everyone is aware is to notify all employees, through whichever media is selected, that their supervisors have been provided with an *action-needed report* for their use.

ACTION NEEDED REPORT

A formal document is required that will provide people with a format with which to convey the problem in a concise and meaningul way. This document must be made available for anyone to use.

Exhibit 6.1 shows a typical action-needed report, which would be accompanied by the following set of instructions. Each report requested by any individual should have a set of instructions attached.

Purpose

"The *action-needed report* is a communication tool designed to provide our employees and supervisors with a formal means of bringing operating problems to the attention of management."

Submitting:

"Anyone can submit a report. If assistance is required, see your immediate supervisor. You may wish to review your report with a supervisor to assure completeness and accuracy. Your participation is appreciated. Please forward through your supervisor (or designated person)."

Completing the Form

1. *Date:* When written.
2. *Originator:* Name of the person suggesting action needed.
3. *A/N#:* Will be assigned by committee Preparer. For committee use.
4. *Description of Problem Requiring Action:* A short, detailed description of the problem.
5. *Recommended Action:* If the originator has ideas for a solution. It is *not* necessary to have a recommended solution to initiate a report.
6. *Estimated Hours or Dollars Lost:* Fill this in only if you have knowledge. Otherwise it will be evaluated later.
7. Remaining spaces are for committee use.

ACTION NEEDED REPORT

DATE

ORIGINATOR	NUMBER	PREPARER

DESCRIPTION OF THE PROBLEM REQUIRING ACTION:

RECOMMENDED ACTION REQUIRED:

ESTIMATED HOURS LOST	ESTIMATED $ LOST/YEAR	APPROVED BY	DATE

ASSIGNED TO	SCHEDULED COMPLETION	ACTUAL COMPLETION

FINAL RESOLUTION OF PROBLEM:

	APPROVED BY	DATE

Exhibit 6–1.

HANDLING THE ACTION-NEEDED REPORT

Upon receipt, the report is put on the agenda for the next committee meeting. A number is assigned to it for control purposes. If the form requires clarification, it is assigned to a committee member for further preparation prior to the meeting. That member then places his name in the preparer box in the upper right. The report may be rewritten by the preparer, but the original should remain attached.

The committee has the responsibility of ensuring that action is taken. For simple problems that can be resolved at the meeting, the final resolution is filled in and a completed copy returned to the *originator* (the person suggesting the action needed). Where possible and practical, a note from the committee chairperson should accompany the form, thanking the originator.

Most problems submitted, more than likely, will require further exploration and perhaps a period of time to arrive at a solution. In these instances, when the recommended action required may not be readily known, the report is assigned to a committee member for further work and a scheduled completion date inserted. In this event, an *action-started* memo, is sent to the originator. See Exhibit 6.2

CONTROLLING THE ACTION-NEEDED REPORTS

Each report submitted should be properly recorded on the committee's log so that control is maintained until completion (Exhibit 6.3). The number assigned is recorded in the left hand column. Next to it a brief description of the problem is inserted, the name of the originator, and the date received.

At the committee meeting, once it has been determined that further work is necessary, a member of the committee is assigned to follow the report through to completion. This person's name is added to the report and entered on the log. At this time, a date for completion is set and the date recorded on the report form and on the log. All of the necessary elements for control now exist. At each meeting of the committee, all open reports on the log are briefly reviewed with the assigned committee member who will update the committee on the progress made or on the lack of progress. Problems inherent in getting answers are discussed and courses of action recommended.

ACTION STARTED MEMO

DATE:_____

NUMBERS:_____

TO_____ DEPARTMENT_____

YOUR **ACTION NEEDED REPORT** REGARDING_____

HAS BEEN ASSIGNED TO MR./MRS./MISS_____

WHO MAY BE CONTACTING YOU DURING THE NEXT FEW DAYS TO GET

YOUR IDEAS FOR CORRECTIVE ACTION OF THE PROBLEM YOU

DESCRIBED. THIS **ACTION NEEDED REPORT** BECOMES DUE FOR AN

ANSWER OR FURTHER STATUS INFORMATION ON _____19___.

_____

Exhibit 6–2.

ACTION NEEDED LOG

ACTION NEEDED NUMBER	DESCRIPTION	ORIGINATOR	DATE RECD	ASSIGNED TO	COMPLETE DATE	
					SCH.	ACCT.

Exhibit 6-3.

Needless to say, if the program is effective, there will probably be a good number of action-needed reports in the committee pipeline. Many of these will have long-range solutions and will remain as open items on the log for a lengthy period of time, so controls become essential to prevent items from being lost or forgotten.

FOLLOW-UP ON OPEN ITEMS

The committee has the responsibility to follow up on every open item until it is resolved or until determination is made that no action can or will be taken. In either situation, it is important that, as part of the follow-up procedure, the originator be kept informed.

The file copy of the action-needed report can be used to record follow-up dates. Assuming the committee meets weekly, every item on the log that has passed its due date and is not listed as having been completed will be reviewed. The file copy is pulled for the meeting.

On those overdue items that have been "pushed out" and a new follow-up date set for the future, assurance is made that the originator has been informed and a brief discussion is conducted on what progress has been made.

Those items that were "pushed out" and are *again overdue* for completion are subjected to further discussion. What or who are the roadblocks? What can be done to overcome them? A plan of action must be laid out. Does this involve inviting some member of management to the committee meeting to prompt his response? If so, do it. In most instances, doing it in writing will encourage action. In every case, when a due date that has been forwarded to the originator has passed without resolution or finalization, that originator must be informed.

An excellent form of follow-up to a recalcitrant member of management is to send the originator a brief memo that the situation has been referred to that particular member for action and that the committee is awaiting his feedback or action. Send a copy of the memo to the manager. There is no need to tell the originator that the individual is not responding. Getting a copy of the delay memo will, very often, produce the desired result. Again, record any action taken on the file copy of the original report.

On items that have become overdue since the last meeting, a discussion with the assigned committee member should prompt the follow-up course of action. Remember to get a follow-up memo out to the originator, which in all cases, should be made out *while the item is being discussed*. Each committee member can make out his own. The memos are then collected by the chairperson who will ensure their delivery to the originator.

EFFECTIVENESS REVIEW

It is almost inevitable, in an organization of any size, that the task of the committee in prompting action and responses from certain departments or individuals will not get results. For this reason, and to keep top management informed, an effectiveness review, on a periodic basis, becomes essential. Here's how it works.

The action-needed chairperson reviews the log once a month. The log will reveal the open items that are more than 45 days old. The files on these are pulled and reviewed. Some of these will have legitimate reasons for their "age," such as long-range solutions. As long as the originator has been properly notified of the time element involved, no further action is needed at this time. The files that reveal a lack of response on the part of any department are kept out for the next committee meeting.

At the meeting, each file is given to the committee member assigned and discussed as to the problem involved. It becomes the responsibility of each individual committee member to follow up. While the meeting is in progress, the committee members will each fill out an *effectiveness review memo* (Exhibit 6.4). Most of these will have been reviewed at prior meetings and some follow-up will have occurred. The purpose here is to put an additional emphasis on getting action.

The committee members will address their review memos to the person or department that is now especially delinquent in responding. If possible, the responsible committee member will personally take the memo to that person or department to have them fill out the bottom portion of the memo, and try to get a firm commitment. Copies of the effectiveness review memo will then be made; one given to the person or department, one to the originator, and, when applicable, one sent to the executive of the company under whom the particular person or department falls.

EFFECTIVENESS REVIEW MEMO

TO: _____

SUBJECT: ACTION NEEDED EFFECTIVENESS REVIEW

ACTION NEEDED #_____ , WHICH WAS SUBMITTED TO YOU/BY YOU,

HAS A PLANNED EFFECTIVENESS REVIEW DATE OF _____

HAS ANYTHING BEEN DONE TO FOLLOW-UP ? HAS THE **ACTION NEEDED**

BEEN RESOLVED TO YOUR SATISFACTION ? DO YOU FEEL THIS PROBLEM

HAS BEEN CORRECTED ?

PLEASE INDICATE IN THE SPACE DESIGNATED BELOW, THE STATUS OF

THE **ACTION NEEDED** AND RETURN IT TO ME SO IT MAY BE CLEARED

FROM THE **ACTION NEEDED LOG BOOK.**

THANK YOU

_____

STATUS OF THE ABOVE **ACTION NEEDED** IS:

_____

_____

_____

_____

_____

_____

_____

_____ SIGNED _____

_____ DATED _____

Exhibit 6–4.

EXECUTIVE INVOLVEMENT

Since the action-needed plan is a company-initiated procedure but is operated by first-line supervision, it must have executive backing. Participation by upper management is twofold. One area of participation, contained in the procedure, is involvement with action-needed requests that come to their level. The plan, of course, is to find the solution to each request at the lowest level possible or practical. The requests are funneled up the line only as the solution requires it. They can reach the top executive level, and those executives are expected to respond just as any other manager or department.

The second way the executive level is involved is to give the action-needed committee the full backing of executive authority in achieving results. In most companies that employ action-needed plans, the executive authority is rarely invoked because the positive nature of the plan stimulates constructive reaction. However, it must be available to the committee as a court of last appeal when a productive response to a particular request has not been obtainable. It is important that everyone who participates by generating a memo eventually receive a final reply. The vast majority of problems, one hopes, will have a positive solution, but even those that cannot be resolved after a full effort should result in a response to the originator with an explanation of the effort that was made and the reason why a solution could not be found.

COMMITTEE MEMBER INSTRUCTIONS

Each member of the committee has the responsibility of handling those action-needed reports assigned to him or her. To function as an effective member of the committee, each member must understand how to proceed.

The first step is to understand the problem as submitted. Is it really a problem or a symptom? Unless the action-needed report is very clear and concise, it may be necessary to get together with the originator to clarify it.

The second step is to determine the causes of the problem. What are they? Where do they originate? Can they be documented? Secure as much information as possible.

Next, determine the severity and frequency of the problem and/or its causes. Can the problem be quantified in terms of lost time, flow interruption, or other types of interferences? Can these be converted to demonstrate a loss in dollars? What efforts in the past, if any, have been made to solve the problem or eliminate the causes?

All of the above are necessary steps prior to attempting to find the solution. The answers should lead the committee member to the person or department most likely to be in a position to work at finding the solution. The action-needed report, with the results of the committee member's efforts, are then forwarded to that person or department. Once the report is taken this far, the follow-up becomes part of the routine function of the committee.

FINISHING THE ACTION-NEEDED REPORT

Before a report is closed out and a completed date is placed on the action-needed log, it must be determined that the problem has actually been solved. The simplest and most direct way is to go back to the originator. Find out if the problem has been eliminated or if the symptoms have just been reduced or hidden. Does the originator indicate satisfaction with the solution?

Follow-up should be made to ensure that the solution to the problem did not create other problems elsewhere. Do not take it for granted that such an outcome was avoided in the development of the solution. Also determine that the solution is permanent and not just a Band-Aid approach. If any of these possibilities exist, the action-needed report remains an open item until the committee and the originator are satisfied. At that point, the report can be closed.

KEEPING UP WITH RESULTS

The most effective action-needed committee will want to report to upper management on the results it is obtaining. Interested management at the executive level will want to be assured that this approach is effective. A simple report, on a monthly or quarterly basis, should provide the ability to communicate results from the committee to the executive level.

Exhibit 6.5 is an example of such a report. It demonstrates the effectiveness of the program in a number of ways. The number of reports submitted shows how people are taking an active interest. The number completed demonstrates the degree of responsiveness

ACTION NEEDED STATUS REPORT

NO   DATE

	THIS MONTH	LAST MONTH	YEAR-TO-DATE
TOTAL ACTION NEEDED REPORTS SUBMITTED			
TOTAL ACTION NEEDED REPORTS COMPLETED			
TOTAL ACTION NEEDED REPORTS NOT SOLVED			

AREA OR DEPARTMENT	TOTAL SUBMITTED	% TOTAL	NUMBER SOLVED	% TOTAL	CLOSED BUT NOT SOLVED

Exhibit 6-5.

by the company. The number remaining unsolved may prompt management to look within itself for the need for action. Breaking the numbers down by area or department of origination to reveal the solutions or lack thereof can assist in the decision-making process and lead to further action at the executive level.

SOME OUTSTANDING RESULTS

In a major oil company, one foreman of an offshore drilling rig made out an action-needed report on his problem of getting prompt delivery of materials from the shorebase. The immediate thought was to add more boats to the service fleet. However, another action-needed memo, generated by a dispatcher, indicated that drilling foremen were delaying boats at the offshore location unnecessarily. Subsequent investigation of both problems revealed that lack of planning and scheduling was the root cause of both problems. This led to the development of a planning, scheduling, and control function that not only solved the problems but reduced costs of the service fleet by more than three million dollars.

A large New England hospital, reacting to a request from a ward clerk that the constant ringing of telephones was not only a distraction but a detriment to efficient operations at the station, replaced the bell ringing with lights. Not only did this cut down on employee turnover, but doctors reported a tremendous decrease in patient complaints about noise.

In one installation and repair station of a major telephone company, an action-needed request initiated by a supervisor, pointed out that so many customer telephone history cards were out of file on a continuing basis that the dispatching of service repairmen was seriously impaired. Subsequent investigation revealed that the condition was prevalent throughout the system. Corrective action resulted in reducing response time on repair calls by more than three hours. The public relations value of this improvement could not be measured in dollars.

Company after company of all types and sizes report amazing results. These results are achieved by initiating a dynamic plan, selling it to the company and the employees, but, most important, implementing the plan as an integral part of company operations and running it in a professional manner.

7

Scheduling and Control Techniques in Direct Labor Operations

Direct labor is that which is applied to the product being manufactured. Machine operators produce parts. Assembly operators put parts together. They perform direct labor. Maintenance operations, shipping and receiving, and material handling are indirect labor. This chapter will deal with direct labor in a manufacturing environment.

BASIC SCHEDULING CONCEPTS

The traditional role of a production control function in a manufacturing company is to plan the amount of product that is to be produced and to establish the ability to produce it. This involves the scheduling of parts to be manufactured, requisitioning purchased parts, loading departments or even machines, and matching production to the capacity of each area and to the plant or to the demands of the market. Production control will issue production orders, keep track of progress, expedite where necessary, and in general manage the "put through" of product. This function is necessary to any company. The scheduling and control techniques that are involved in this chapter are either an extension of that effort or, in some cases, can become an integral part of it. The concept involved in these techniques is to provide the first-line supervisor with tools and training that will give him more control over his immediate operations.

THE NECESSARY INGREDIENTS

In the chapter on training supervision, it was pointed out that the supervisor must be given information that is meaningful to him and must be taught the meaning and application of that information to his operation. Simply stated, he must be able to control his resources. He has certain "needs to know." These are: what has to be produced, the method of production, the resources available (i.e. the tools, equipment, and machinery to produce it), and the amount of labor required.

There must be a flow of material into the department, a system for putting that material into and through the department, and removing the end product to another area. With rare exceptions, this requires paperwork. It is often said that to control the flow of parts and material, one must control the paperwork.

With all of the above being true, what additional ingredient is required? None, if the company is not concerned with the loss of profit that is inherent in most operations because the foreman has not been given the ultimate tools of resource management. These tools are a tangible means to define and correct conditions that are interfering with good production on a current basis. When these have been put in place and the foreman taught how to use them, then he is in a position to best produce results with optimum cost effectiveness.

DETAILED ANALYTICAL PHASE

In approaching any department with the thought of providing tools of control, the person assigned to the department must first go through a development process. This is the detailed analytical phase as described in the schedule. There is a definite procedure. Assumption is made here that the first general phase (introductory) has been completed as previously described.

First, it is best to get a detailed, scale layout of the department. If one is not available, then a reasonably accurate drawing of the department must be made. In either case, every piece of machinery and equipment must be shown. If a drawing from engineering is used, its accuracy must be verified. This can be readily accomplished by visual inspection.

The next step is to understand the flow or flows of work through the department. This understanding is developed through learning the paperwork process in detail and by physically walking the flow.

Once this is accomplished, the processes of determining the proper staffing and developing the means of control can begin. Because it is impossible to describe, in one chapter, the application of controls to the vast variety of manufacturing situations, we will try to present general examples that the reader may apply to specific situations.

INDIVIDUAL MACHINE OPERATIONS

Individual machine operations, a type of manufacture that will be found in a sheet metal fabrication or a press department, require that the supervisor have the ability to control every operation through every piece of equipment. He must be able to plan the utilization of machines and the assignment of people to the machines. He will be dealing with a variety of skills such as punch press operators, drill operators, and so forth. The control of these operations starts with the manufacturing process card, the document, usually issued by production control, that causes the material to be drawn from storage and moved to the department in which the first process step will take place.

The process card must give the foreman the necessary detail to control his operations. It will contain each process step in sequence, describe each step, and list the type of equipment that the step will be performed on and the tooling or fixturing required. It will list the quantity of the part to be produced. In companies that have engineered time studies, the rate at which the job will run at each given step will be listed. This is generally used as a means of after-the-fact evaluation of production efficiency and as such has minimal value to the foreman. The process card must be expanded to include additional data.

First of all, the rate or time per piece, usually expressed in a three or four decimal number must be applied against the order quantity to come up with a *run-time* at each process step. A simple change in format can accomplish this. In addition, a setup time for each process step should be included, as applicable. With this data on the card, the foreman has the necessary information to plan his work on a continuing basis. Exhibit 7.1 shows a fabrication shop order that provides the necessary data to the foreman.

Fabrication Shop Order No.				Issue Date				Card 1 of 2	
								Card Quantity 200	
Part Number A6437-2L			Part Name Hinge			Material I.D. Stock #42765SS		Total Order 400	
Step II	OP #	Dept.	Operation Description		Tool I.D.	S.U. time	Rate	Run time	Plan Date
1	201	32	Mill 3/8" Round Per Drawing 42765		NA	.2hrs	50hr	4hrs	6/29
2	216	32	Drill 8 Holes Per Drawing 42765		523 M 8	.3hrs	35hr	5.7hrs	6/30
3	430	46	Bend–Offcenter By ¼" Per Drawing 42765		600 F 16	.2hrs	45hr	4.4hrs	7/1

Exhibit 7-1.

Note that all of the basic data are shown.

- Part identification
- Quantity
- Material required
- Department(s) in which the operations will be performed

- Each operation in sequence
- Tooling required for each operation
- Setup time
- Run-time (quantity × rate)

The quantity to be produced is equal to the capacity of the container used to transport the material through the flow. Quantities are produced in multiples of the container with an additional card issued for each container amount. The card travels with the material, which provides the capacity to move containers ahead to the next operation and thus to put large jobs through on a more horizontal than vertical basis. This methodology improves the flow and reduces the time in process, which in turn reduces in-process inventories. It also provides the ability to expedite the process when necessary by using several pieces of equipment at the same time (assuming the availability of duplicate tooling).

STAGING REQUIREMENTS

The next step may be more difficult: the staging of materials in front of the department and the staging of the job in process at each step through the department. Proper staging is critical to the process flow. Sufficient space must be provided, which means, ideally, that there should be sufficient space at each machine to handle the current job and at least one back-up job. Once a job is entered into the department, it should move from operation to operation in a smooth consistent flow. The more time spent in waiting between process steps, the higher the cost of in-process inventory.

In a midwest manufacturing cmpany that produces brake master cylinders for the OEM and aftermarket of the automobile industry, the cost of in-process inventory was crippling the profit picture. Each area, from raw castings to the final assembly operation was jammed with work in process. Material movement was a nightmare. Four separate departments were involved. The institution of a control system reduced the in-process inventory by 54%, opened up space for good staging, and reduced the time in process by more than one third.

With the process cards set up to give the foreman the needed time elements and with the staging areas and equipment in the best possible locations to accommodate the flow, the means by which the foreman controls the operation must then be developed. In many cases, control can be accomplished prior to the improvement in the staging and, of itself, will assist in reducing staging space requirements, making room for additional improvements. The formats of control can vary and will depend upon the ability of the coordinator and the foreman to mutually *imagineer* them. Here are some methods that have been used successfully.

LOG CONTROL

As each day's work is planned, the jobs are entered on a log. The jobs are listed in the left-hand column by part number. Each process step is listed by sequential number under a machine in the proper grouping. The setup time is shown directly under the sequence step and the run-time under that.

The method is illustrated by Exhibit 7.2, which demonstrates several things. For example, part no. 24615 is scheduled at drill press no. 2 for its first operation. The setup time and run-time show that drill press no. 2 will be tied up for 2.2 hours (setup plus run-time). The same holds true for punch press no. 3 and forming press no. 1. Note that forming press no. 3 is shown as an alternate.

Part no. 26512 starts out with operation 1 at punch press no. 1. The second operation in this two-step process is at drill press no. 4. As each job is added, it is relatively simple to keep track of the load on each machine by distributing the load across each machine group. In this type of scheduling, the foreman must distribute the work by machine but must load the machines *and* the operators. He cannot load any one machine greater than its capacity nor any group of

PRESS DEPARTMENT

DAILY MACHINE SCHEDULE

PART #		MACHINE GROUPINGS – PROCESS STEPS										
		DRILL PRESSES				PUNCH PRESSES				FORMING PRESSES		
		1	2	3	4	1	2	3	4	1	2	3
24615	OP#		①					②		③		④
	S.U.		.2					.4		.3		
	RUN		2.2					2.6		1.6		
26512	OP#				②	①						
	S.U.				.3	.1						
	RUN				1.8	1.3						
	OP#											

Exhibit 7–2.

machines greater than the capacity of the number of available operators.

This method is simple and assists the foreman in planning machine and labor utilization. It is somewhat loose in that it does not control the job movement from one process step to another. The control is effective in relatively small fabrication departments where the foreman has a lot of visual control and can physically direct the material movement. In larger departments of this type, the next method, though more involved, may better serve the purpose.

MACHINE LOAD SEQUENCING

In larger and more complex operations, the sequencing of each job through the flow will bring about a better ability to control the department. In this type of control, each job's operations are planned to move in specific time periods. Exhibit 7.3 is a typical flow pattern.

The machines are listed down the left by group. The time bar across the top represents the shift hours. Note that 15 minutes has been deleted between 9:00 and 10:00 in the morning and between 1:00 and 2:00 in the afternoon, representing relief breaks. The half hour lunch break has been deleted between 11:00 and 12:00. For the illustration, a paper schedule is shown. A magnetic or chalk board could also be used.

Part no. 3162 has been scheduled for milling machine no. 1. The combined setup and run-time is scheduled for two and one half hours (.25 hr s.u. + 2.25 hr run). With a quarter hour for movement from the mills to the drills, the same part has been scheduled into drill no. 3 where the prior scheduled part was completed an hour earlier. The final operation is scheduled into punch press no. 3. Each of the parts scheduled follows the same pattern. With this type scheduling, maximum use of the equipment is attained and the in-process inventory is minimized. In most shops, there are more machines than men. With this scheduling a proper balance is attained.

MAKING THINGS HAPPEN

Laying out a plan is only the beginning of the job. It can be expected that things will go wrong, and the plan will go awry on numerous occasions. The job of the foreman is to be alert to take timely cor-

PRESS DEPARTMENT SCHEDULE

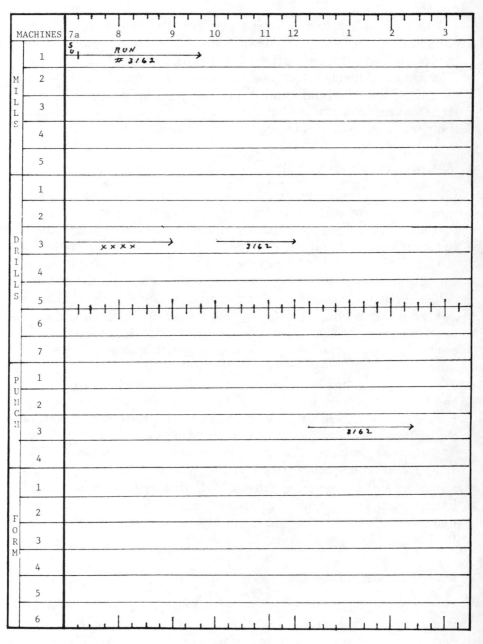

Exhibit 7–3.

rective action, minimize lost machine and man time, and keep the flow going. Each of the above methods provides him with the necessary visual knowledge of what *should* happen. When things go wrong, the sooner he recognizes that fact, the sooner he can correct the problem. The points in time for completion of each job provide check points for him. If the short-range goal has not been achieved, he can, on a timely basis, recognize that fact, take corrective or remedial action, and minimize the loss of productive capacity.

SIMULTANEOUS MACHINE OPERATIONS

Many manufacturing organizations have departments where one operator controls several automatic or semiautomatic machines. These present a different set of circumstances. The machines will each be doing a sequential process step to a product. Many assembly and/or subassembly operations are of this nature. The output is continuous and does not lend itself to the controls described above.

However, in these operations, work has been related to time, the machines have been geared to a given rate of output, and production goals have been established. The problems arise when production goals are not met and the cost per unit of production goes up. The work and its related elements must be controlled on some short interval basis. Each part or element must be controlled in order to control the whole. All variances from the norm must be recognized and investigated immediately for prompt identification of the problem causing the variance. The solutions that are then developed can be of an immediate nature to minimize the loss at the moment and/or of a long-range nature of corrective action to prevent recurrences.

What must be done in this type of operation is to develop logical check points on a short-interval basis that will measure the output. It is too late, at the end of a shift to know that a machine group fell several thousand units short of the production goal because of a condition that developed early in the day. Had the condition been recognized earlier, many hours of lost production could have been salvaged.

The goal here is to provide an early warning system, one that will alert the foreman to a condition that is interrupting or slowing down

MACHINE GROUP PRODUCTION CHECKS

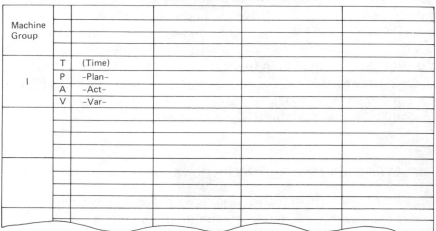

Machine Group						
I	T	(Time)				
	P	–Plan–				
	A	–Act–				
	V	–Var–				

Exhibit 7–4.

his production. The key is taking production readings from the machines on a regular basis. The frequency of the readings can be hourly or every two hours, depending on the critical nature or the cost of the part. This can usually be accomplished by a clerk whose job requires that he take the readings on a routine basis.

At each machine group, the clerk takes the reading and records the production and the lapsed time (since the start or the last reading). He then calculates the standard production rate for the same period and compares the two. If the actual production is less than the standard by more than a predetermined percentage, the clerk records the information on a *schedule variance report,* which is given immediately to the foreman for investigation and corrective action. The clerk retains a copy in an open file as a check against lost or unreported variance reports.

Exhibit 7.4 is an example of the recording mechanism that the clerk can use to make the rounds of the machines. The clerk records the time T that the reading was taken and inserts the quantity produced as of that point in time, A. He also inserts the standard or plan time P, calculated by the rate of production multiplied by the lapsed time. The plus or minus difference is figured and the foreman is immediately informed of any variance.

SCHEDULE VARIANCE REPORT

The means of informing the foreman and his subsequent action is the key to the cost reduction effort. His timely knowledge that something is wrong gives him the opportunity to take immediate corrective action, minimize the loss, and readjust his schedule if required. On repetitive-type problems he may want to utilize the action-needed format to secure action that will bring about a long-range solution. This type of variance reporting has a number of advantages (see Exhibit 7.5).

First of all, it requires an action on the part of the foreman. He has no choice but to investigate the cause of the variance. By so doing, he will uncover many things that interfere with good production. Second, by having him record the nature of the problem and what action he took for an immediate solution as well as the results achieved, he exposes his judgement, his knowledge of his operations, and his problem-solving ability. These factors open doors of communication between the foreman and his superior for improving performance.

	Schedule Variance Report				
Department		Machine Group		Date	
Time of Reading	Plan Count	Actual Count	Variance	Time	Reported By
Cause of Variance:					
Action Taken–Results:					
Action Needed:					
				Foreman:	

Exhibit 7–5.

The third advantage is the documenting of problems that are recurring and have, historically, been a cause of lost time in the operation. The fact that the loss is measured provides the ability to cost out the value of the loss and compare it to the cost of the correction required. This is of particular value when expensive tooling is involved.

Another type of control, effective in operations involving a number of people, each one of whose performance can be measured against different quantities and standards, is to create a visual mechanism to provide the foreman with the early warning. This type of control is relatively simple and very effective.

A case in point is the test department of a medium-sized manufacturer of circuit protection devices. These devices vary in size and shape, and their electromechanical operations have several variables. Each order consists of a number of the product of a certain dimension and configuration. Each piece requires a test, performed by individuals seated at electromechanical test sets. Each order will vary in both quantity and test requirements and therefore can take a different amount of time. With about 35 people involved under 1 foreman, to control each on a continuing basis appears to be a formidable challenge.

The initial step was to convert each order into a testing time by multiplying the standard test time by the quantity. This information appeared on the process card. Next, a board was constructed with pockets to accept the control copy of the order. The board was constructed so that a series of eight pockets were fitted across the horizontal, representing the work hours for the individual employees, whose names appeared down the vertical on the left.

On assignment of each order to a tester, the foreman would pull his control copy. He would add the testing time shown to the time of assignment and insert the copy in the pocket opposite the person assigned and under the time period at which the job should be completed. With all currently assigned jobs in place, he could visually ascertain which orders were due for completion at various hours during the day. He could start with those that had the earliest due completion times and check on their progress. This provided a means of setting priorities for the movements through the department.

As each order was completed, the material handler would retrieve the control copy from the board. In this manner, any copy left on the board at the end of its completion hour would serve as a flag that a variance would occur. The foreman had only to glance at the board and know where his attention should be directed. He could then investigate, take corrective action, and minimize his variances.

Since this type of control has a high degree of visibility, each person in the department was aware of the completion time. The psychological advantage of this awareness had a twofold benefit. It practically eliminated people problems as a cause of variances and resulted, very often, in individuals bringing problems of material or test set failures to the foreman's attention even before the due time of completion.

The one compromise that material control had to make to enable it to function was to divide large orders into increments of no more than two hours. This proved to have an additional beneficial effect in that the foreman could assign large orders to several test sets, reducing the time in process, speeding delivery, and reducing the amount of in-process inventory.

SUMMARY

In direct labor operations, the program's application is at the foreman level. He must be provided with the tools to control his resources, plan his work, execute the plan, and recognize when things are not going according to plan. When aware of problems, he must take corrective action, record what he did, and request help on problems that are beyond his scope to solve on the spot. The result is better utilization of personnel, increased productivity, and reduction of unit cost. In addition, delivery times are shortened, material in process decreased, and a higher predictability of results achieved.

8

Scheduling and Controlling
Maintenance Operations

In many companies, the utilization of labor hours in the indirect areas of labor receives very little attention. Because these areas are not readily adaptable to traditional work measurement techniques, they are considered beyond the scope of labor cost control. As a result, they are budgeted poorly and are often subjected to inequitable decisions relating to the actual need of the facility for their services.

Maintenance departments are probably the most vulnerable on this score. Decisions on the size of the maintenance force are rarely made based on an accurate calculation of real need. Maintenance departments, in the minds of most maintenance superintendents, are understaffed. The other departments, which rely on maintenance for service, are often unhappy with the lack of response to what they consider their best interests.

This chapter will explain how to reduce the costs of maintenance through better utilization of manpower and how to establish a control that will clearly establish maintenance manpower requirements and assure an improvement in service.

TYPES OF MAINTENANCE

With few exceptions, maintenance work can be classified as:

Emergency: That which demands immediate response
Preventive: Periodic specific work on equipment or facilities

Routine: Usually that which follows a route doing a specific type of work on a planned frequency

Reactive: Daily inputs of work requests from outside of the department; can be subclassified by priority and by craft, as applicable

Project: Major work involving building renovation, installation, etc., requiring many hours of work over a lengthy period of time

All of these types of maintenance must be integrated into the control program.

ASSIGNING WORK PRIORITIES

The demands placed upon the maintenance facility by any individual department are usually of high priority to that department. It is the tendency of many department heads to exaggerate the degree of priority for their requests, even to the point of indicating an emergency or priority 1 for many items that do not qualify. To assist the overall effort, priority definitions should be established so that everyone requesting maintenance services evaluates need in the same way. This can be as simple as a five-step priority system such as this:

1. Emergency: Indicates an immediate danger to life or limb or threat of production shutdown
2. Immediate: Will become an emergency if not handled within 24 hours
3. Important: Will be required for meeting a specific need within a week
4. Needed: Indicates desired work that can be accomplished within a month
5. Deferrable: Indicates work that is nonessential and can be done as time permits, usually two to three months

In the larger and more complex organizations, a more sophisticated priority system may be required. Exhibit 8.1 is an example of a priority matrix designed for a large plant with a maintenance work force of over 1000 people.

The priority system serves several purposes. It provides each user a means of qualifying his need in line with everyone else's. It enables the maintenance department to work from its backlog in a more pre-

MAINTENANCE WORK REQUEST PRIORITY MATRIX

CATEGORY	A SAFETY	B PRODUCTION CONTROL PRODUCT QUALITY ENERGY CONSERVATION	C MORALE LABOR RELATIONS PUBLIC RELATIONS
1 EMERGENCY Immediate Response of All Necessary Resources Without Limitation.	Physical damage to employees	Visibility of absolute destruction of property and facilities Failure that will seriously affect production or product quality	
2 URGENT A. Work is essential to prevent emergency condition. B. Work is to be scheduled within 48 hours.	Potential hazard that may result in the destruction of property and will get worse if not corrected.	Failure that could possible result in serious production and quality deficiencies if not corrected.	Failure that impairs production of a process area other than the originator's.
3 SHORT RANGE A. Work required to optimize efficiency of effort and to assure completion by data required. B. Work is to be scheduled within one week.		Repairs and projects to improve costs, increase production, improve quality and/or conserve energy.	Work necessary to meet contractual agreements and/or maintain morale and employee relations.
4 DEFERRED Priority 2 or 3 work Pending equipment availability		MAINTENANCE USE ONLY	
5 LONG RANGE A. Work requested by management affecting long range operation of facilities. B. Work is scheduled to meet calendar requirements.	Projects and preventative work to eliminate potential problems.	Preventative work and long range projects related to production costs, energy conservation or quality improvements.	Repairs and projects for employee facilities and public relations.
6 NON-WORKABLE Priority 2 or 3 work pending availability or parts, tools, materials and/or drawings required		MAINTENANCE USE ONLY	

Exhibit 8-1.

cise manner. It will also, as will be demonstrated later in the chapter, assist in keeping the maintenance work force in line with the real needs of the company.

RELATING WORK TO TIME

As in any scheduling and control system involving the use of labor, it is necessary to relate the work to be done to the hours required to do it. In the maintenance department, it will be found that the major part of the work will be in the reactive area. This is usually nonrepetitive work that does not lend itself to work measurement.

Preventive maintenance (PM) items are repetitive. A PM program is normally well defined, and each PM item, regardless of how the system is set up, will be defined in specific terms and frequencies. In order to integrate the preventive maintenance into the scheduling and control system, it is necessary only to attach an element of time to each PM item. For example, in a midwest bakery, the program for preventive maintenance is a manual card system. Each PM activity or item is on an individual card on which the procedural steps are spelled out. The person performing the work checks off each item as he progresses. A block was added to the card for insertion of the time required to perform the task. Observations were taken on those activities performed on a weekly and monthly basis and the time added to the card system. On those items performed less frequently, an estimate by the supervisor was used. Each routine item can be handled in the same manner.

Reactive-type maintenance presents a different situation since each item is individual and unique. A work order system lends itself to a procedure of estimating the labor required. Estimates will be applied by a knowledgeable person, usually the foreman. In some companies, all work orders go through an estimating group whose job is to establish the time required to perform the related tasks.

Project work is more complex but an estimate of the labor hours required by craft for each phase of the project can be made.

PLAN TIME VERSUS ACTUAL TIME

A key element of a good control is the matching of the time elements as defined to the actual time consumed in the performance of the work. The plan time elements will enable the responsible person to

RUNNING MAINTENANCE	Glycol Pumps (Union TX-10			MECHANIC	DATE	CARD NO

CHECK/PERFORM FOLLOWING FUNCTIONS. CORRECT AS NEEDED. INDICATE COMPLETION WITH "X" IN APPROPRIATE BLOCK.

1. Discharge pressure normal?
2. Crankcase oil level OK?
3. Gear case oil level OK?
4. Lubricator oil reservoir level OK?
5. Plunger packing leakage excessive?
6.
7.
8.
9.
10.

11.
12.
13.
14.
15.
16.
17.
18.
19.
20.

Plan Time
.3 Hrs.
Actual Time
_____

Exhibit 8–2.

properly track the work load and to assign work with an idea of what performance to expect. The feedback of actual performance is equally important in order to measure results.

Exhibit 8.2 is an example of a preventive maintenance card on

JOB REQUEST

DATE 4/15	REQUESTED BY HODGEKINS	Priority: _1_
EQUIPMENT Flow Control Valve - Line 3		Est Hrs: _2.5_
		Act Hrs: _2.75_

INDICATED TROUBLE   Fluttering Noise in Valve
(Pressure and Flow O.K.)

MAINTENANCE REPORT

DISPOSITION
☒ REPAIRED   ☐ REPLACED   NO REPAIR ☐ NEEDED   (SEE REMARKS)

REMARKS   *REPLACED DIAPHRAGM*

DATE 4/17	REPAIRMAN MIKE	FOREMAN Jim Castle

Note: – Priority inserted by requestor
        – Estimated hours inserted by foreman
        – Actual hours inserted by repairman

Exhibit 8–3.

which the plan time has been posted and provision made to receive feedback of the actual time.

Exhibit 8.3 is an example of a completed work order ticket designed to have the work order estimated and the actual time posted. With the above elements (setting priorities, plan time, and actual time) in place, the system can be developed.

METHODS TO CONTROL PAPERWORK

The starting point of the system is to set up the flow of paperwork and the necessary means to control it. The responsibility for control will vary with the size and scope of the department. The most difficult paper to control is the work order. It must be controlled from the point of origination through execution and on to completion. At least three copies of the work order, which consists of a multiple part form, are required.

The original copy travels the farthest and should be made of a paper stock that will withstand a lot of handling. The second copy remains with the original until the point of assignment of the order to the craftsman. The third copy remains with the originator. Additional copies may be required in maintenance operations that frequently have several crafts involved on the same order or in situations where a copy of the order is used as a purchase requisition.

Exhibit 8.4 describes the flow of a normal three-part work order. The flow is rather simple and straightforward. The originator removes and files his copy, forwarding two copies to the maintenance department.

Upon receipt, maintenance estimates the work order and logs it in (see Exhibit 8.5 for a sample of a typical log). The log is essential to guard against lost work orders and also serves as an easy method for recapping backlogs and recording actual hours.

The order then goes in one of two directions. If it can be worked on, it goes into the file of available work. If it must be held for the arrival of parts, it goes into a nonavailable file, usually one set up as a tickler-type system for parts expediting.

From the file of available work, the work order goes into the weekly plan file. Upon assignment, the original copy goes with the person assigned to perform the work. The second copy remains in the foreman's control file, to be matched up with the original upon return and eventually to be placed in a completed file.

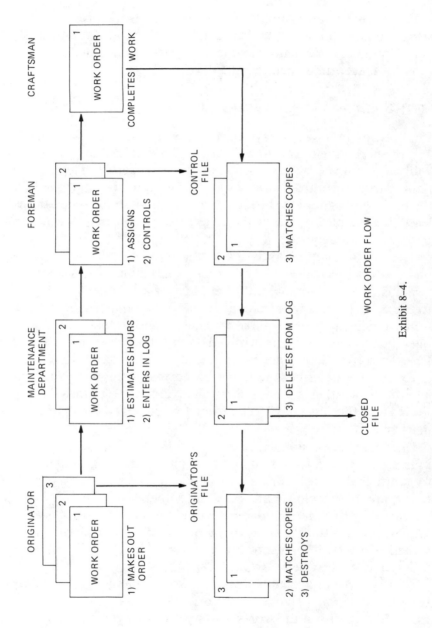

Exhibit 8-4.

MAINTENANCE ORDER LOG

PRIORITY _____
SHOP _____
PLANT _____

Log No.	Date	Charge No.	Job Description	MECH		ELECT		P/F		TOTAL
				Est.	Act.	Est.	Act.	Est.	Act.	

Exhibit 8–5.

The handling of the preventive and routine maintenance systems is usually much simpler because they are an integral part of maintenance. In large companies, however, the systems can be more complex. These items do not go through the logging procedure but proceed to the foreman. What is released to the foreman should be those items required for the coming week.

KEEPING TRACK OF THE BACKLOG

The introduction of a backlog control enables an ongoing determination of the amount of work in the department or a section. This can be continuously measured against the availability of labor hours to perform the work and is the key to maintaining the proper economic staffing level.

There are two aspects to the backlog. The first is work that is available to the department to do. The other is work that has been entered but that cannot be worked on until sometime in the future for any of a variety of reasons. The unavailable backlog is strictly a memo figure to be considered when making future staffing plans.

The backlog procedure is designed to capture hours of work and interpret them in a weekly labor requirement that will keep the backlog in line with a predetermined position. It provides the ability to adjust staffing and priority time parameters and signals that the staffing of the department is or is not at the proper economic level.

Exhibit 8.6 is an example of a backlog report. The following is a step-by-step instruction for its completion.

First, the hours carried forward from the prior week for each priority of work and any preventive or routine jobs are inserted along the "beginning backlog" line.

On a daily basis, enter the estimated hours of work received, by priority. The entire week's input of preventive or routine maintenance is entered on Monday.

Each day enter the estimated hours of completed work orders and preventive or routine items completed.

Add the hours received to the prior day's carried hours and deduct the hours completed to get the current day's carried hours.

Friday's carried hours become the following week's beginning backlog.

BACKLOG REPORT

Priority	1	2	3	4	P.M. Routine	Total
Beginning Backlog						
MONDAY — Received						
MONDAY — Completed						
MONDAY — Carried						
TUESDAY — Received						
TUESDAY — Completed						
TUESDAY — Carried						
WEDNESDAY — Received						
WEDNESDAY — Completed						
WEDNESDAY — Carried						
THURSDAY — Received						
THURSDAY — Completed						
THURSDAY — Carried						
FRIDAY — Received						
FRIDAY — Completed						
FRIDAY — Carried						

Exhibit 8–6.

The tracking of the hours by priority each day will ensure proper attention to each category. The Friday carried will also be the key to the backlog calculations on the management report described later in this chapter.

WEEKLY MAINTENANCE PLAN

A weekly plan is required in those maintenance departments that work from a heavy backlog. Considerable planning should go into the decision process of selecting the right work. Each backlog priority must be kept in line with the priority goals. In smaller maintenance organizations, the work can be selected directly from the log and daily assignments made.

In the planning process, the foreman or planner selects work *to fill up the available hours* of his personnel. In most instances he starts with a basic 40 hour week, deducts known absences, makes allow-

WEEKLY MAINTENANCE PLAN			Week of _____ Craft _____			
No. of Craftsmen Assigned _____ X 37.5 Hours = _____ Gross Hours No. of Days Plan Vac./ABS_____ X 7.5 Hours = _____ Loss Hours Available Hours						
LOG #	# CHARGE	DESCRIPTION/LOCATION		Est. Hours	Cum. Hours	Act. Hours

Exhibit 8-7.

ances for break and washup, and loads to 100% of the remaining time. His plan for the week's work for each craft, group, or individual will vary by the complexity and flexibility of the department.

This planning function can be accomplished in one of two ways. The actual work order, routine card, or preventive maintenance ticket can be pulled from the file as the hours are totaled from the backlog report and filed by craft, group, or individual. The other method is to make out a weekly plan as shown in Exhibit 8.7.

In either case, the foreman or planner accumulates the estimated hours until he has fully loaded the craft, group, or individual. The form also provides for the feedback of actual hours spent in accomplishing each job.

The use of a weekly planning form has a number of advantages. It ensures the ability to fully load the facility. It provides an easy vehicle to show changes in the plan, and it also provides an easy means of recapping the week's results for reporting purposes.

DAILY WORK ASSIGNMENTS

It is the responsibility of the foreman to manage the time of his people. The recording and planning functions that have been demonstrated up to this point must now come to fruition in the work assignment and control procedure.

The foreman assigns work on a daily basis from the plan or from the backlog. His basic assignments consist of work orders, routine slips, and/or preventive maintenance cards, each of which has a time requirement. The foreman can thus make work assignments in terms of time by loading each individual with a full day's work.

He can elect to give all or some of his people one or two assignments of less than a full day's work. In such cases, he must have a means of knowing when such assignments should be completed and have the next assignment ready for those people.

In both cases, the foreman must have a means of knowing where his people are, what they are doing, when they can be expected to be completed with the assigned work. The methods to accomplish this are many and varied, but the use of *a* method is essential. It is the essence of control.

METHODS OF CONTROL

A method popular with a lot of foremen is to use a pigeon hole arrangement. This enables them to exercise the necessary control without incurring additional paperwork. A rack of pigeon holes can be constructed with a two-part pigeon hole for each man. In the planning stage, the foreman places the work orders, cards etc. in the *plan* hole. When the worker is actually assigned, he is given the card, work order copy and is on his way. The copy of each remains in the *at work* hole in the order in which they will be accomplished. This will enable the foreman to readily check on progress throughout the day. When he elects to give out less than a day's work, he must have a means of knowing when the individual should report back for additional work. This can be accomplished by attaching a flag to the *at work* hole indicating the time due back.

Another method of control is an assignment sheet showing the individual's name, a list of his assignments and locations in consecutive order of priority, and the time for each. It becomes a simple matter to determine where the man *should* be at any point in time. This format can also include space to post the actual time for each job against the estimated time for recap purposes.

One control format that is quite effective and has the additional advantage of creating a consciousness on the part of each member of the department or craft is a sign-out blackboard. Upon receipt of his work, each worker lists on the board, in space under his name, the location of each of his assignments and indicates the time (from–to) that he plans to be in each location. This format can be further simplified by having the board printed with the names of the personnel across the top and a time scale down the left hand side. The men can then list the locations and draw a line across corresponding to the time scale.

FOREMAN FOLLOW-UP

Up to this point, we have developed a situation wherein all work is logged, counted, and assigned on the basis of time. This is the beginning of the function of time management. The tools are in place. The actual use of the tools by the foreman brings the entire procedure full circle and begins to make things happen.

First of all, the planning stage should ensure that no work is assigned unless the availability of parts, tools, and the equipment or machinery to be worked on has been determined. The work assignment and control procedure set the stage for the foreman to know where his people are, what they are doing, and when they should be finished.

The second stage of foreman follow-up is the preparation and planning of the next round of work. This can be accomplished once all current assignments are in motion.

Stage three is the actual follow-up. The foreman must get out of his office and into the work area. He has the tools in place to readily locate his people and determine that their work is progressing, offering his advice and expertise as he proceeds and recognizing that work assignments are proceeding as planned.

This kind of follow-up will be recognized immediately by the work force. They will know that the time expectations are important and that the boss is serious in his anticipations of workload completion. They will soon become aware that *excuses* for not completing assignments will not hold up but that legitimate reasons for delays will be dealt with effectively.

SCHEDULE DELAY HANDLING

Perhaps the most important part of the foreman's follow-up is the recognition and handling of problems that interfere with the progress of work. He begins to recognize these through his follow-up procedure. His men will also become more aware of these causes of delay and will report them to him.

A common occurrence in manufacturing plants is the failure on the part of production to make a piece of machinery available to maintenance on a specific day with sufficient time to do minor repairs. Inevitably, the repairman arrives and will waste from a few minutes to several hours waiting. This has always been an accepted situation until the time elements involved are recognized and follow-up takes place. It is an easily correctable item that historically has resulted in lost maintenance man-hours that can be put to productive use.

The list of things can go on and on. The efforts at seeking corrective action are endless. In order to keep this an active and ongoing procedure, certain rules can be established and a mechanism created to ensure compliance.

THE SCHEDULE DELAY REPORT

The rule can be simple. Every time a job assignment is missed by an excess of 10% of the estimated or standard time, the foreman makes out a *schedule delay report.*
The information required in the report is simple:

- Day and date of occurrence
- Description of job involved (brief)
- Estimated hours to complete
- Actual hours spent
- Cause of the delay
- Corrective action taken to avoid recurrence or minimize lost time

This puts a requirement on the foreman to be alert to problems and to be a problem solver. He becomes more and more aware of the opportunities to minimize delays and make his people more productive. When he incurs problems of a serious nature that are beyond his expertise or authority, he has only to put them into the action-needed program.

MAINTENANCE REPORTING

In a good cost reduction/productivity improvement program in a maintenance department, the key to success lies with the foreman and his ability to plan, assign, and follow up. The entire program, of course, must include the ability to manage the overall workload and manpower requirements of the department to make certain that the department is properly staffed and functioning efficiently. For management to be able to do this effectively, they must have certain information on a continuing basis. The information can vary from one maintenance department to another but must contain certain details:

- How does the work load match the work force?
- Is the backlog of work in proper perspective?

- Are maintenance personnel being utilized effectively?
- Are maintenance operations as productive as practical?

All of the information that is necessary will come out of the installed procedures outlined in this chapter. It is now a matter of putting together a concise report that will inform management of the status on a weekly basis. This report can be generated manually, but if all of the elements of control have been programmed into a computer, the report can be generated by the computer. It is recommended that the report be generated on a weekly basis.

THE MAINTENANCE REPORT

Exhibit 8.8 represents a typical maintenance report by craft. Here is how it works and what it means. Note that although it is set up by craft, departmental totals can be drawn.

The left side of the report gives a backlog status by priority and in total for the craft. Each priority represents a time period, established by management and measured in calendar weeks, within which the amount of hours in the backlog should be completed. This is an important facet of determining staffing requirements.

The percentage productivity on the left represents a five week rolling average of the productivity of the craft.

To a beginning backlog of hours listed by priority and in total, all incoming hours are added for the week. This information comes from the maintenance log and preventive and routine maintenance cards scheduled for the week. All completed work, again from the maintenance log, is totaled. Note that in both the work received and completed blocks, we are dealing with the estimated or established hours and not with the actual hours.

To the beginning backlog, add the incoming hours, subtract the completed hours and post the ending backlog hours.

Divide the ending backlog hours for each priority by the weeks established for completion. This represents the labor hours required per week to remain on top of the backlog.

Since estimating is an inexact science and since performance can vary, the five week running average of productivity will also serve as a determining factor.

CRAFT		BACKLOG DATA AND WORKLOAD STATUS										CURRENT WEEK'S PERFORMANCE					
	P	BEG. B.L.	RCVD.	COMP.	END B.L.	WKS. TO	HRS. REQ.	% PROD.	NET HRS.	HRS. AVAIL.	+ − VAR.	HOURS PROD-UCED	HOURS USED	% PROD-UCTIVE	HOURS WORKED	% UTILIZ.
	1															
	2															
	3															
	4															
	T															

Exhibit 8-8.

Multiply the total of the hours required by the productivity factor and post the total *net hour required*. This adjustment brings the requirement into line with results being achieved. Next, plug in the weekly hours available. This would be the number of people on the staff multiplied by the net hours per person available for work, normally 37.5 hours.

The difference between the two figures on a plus or minus basis demonstrates whether or not the staff and the workload are in line. It enables management to maintain the proper economic staffing level.

The right-hand portion of the report reflects the results for the week. The estimated hours and the actual hours *from completed work only* are posted. Productivity is calculated by dividing the estimated hours by the actual.

To determine the utilization, insert the total hours worked. Divide the actual hours from the completed work by the total hours worked to calculate this percentage. Recognize that the actual hours worked on completed work will not represent all of the hours since there will be hours spent on incomplete work. This figure is a barometer of utilization and not an exact figure. It will serve as an *indicator* of how well the work force is being used on an ongoing basis.

SUMMARY

By gaining control over the work load in terms of hours, by using these hours to manage the time of the work force, following up as required and constantly seeking corrective action to eliminate causes of delays and minimizing interfering influence, management can keep the maintenance work force at the peak of performance. By the diligent use of the data generated by the controls, the maintenance work force can be kept in line with the real need of the facility. This combination will assure that costs are in line and the service is such that the manufacturing facility will operate at its best level of performance.

9

Scheduling and Controlling Other Areas of Indirect Labor

Areas of indirect labor, such as the shipping, receiving and warehouse functions, custodial services, and quality control, offer excellent opportunities for cost reduction. Since these areas are normally neglected from the viewpoint of work measurement, they are, most often, overstaffed and underproductive.

Such a statement, which may appear harsh and condemning to managers of such departments, is not meant to be. Managers of these areas are usually expert in their fields from long years of service. Since they are seldom, if ever, exposed to the concept of relating work requirements to labor hours, they cannot be expected to think in such terms. This chapter will be devoted to ideas, methods, and techniques that can assist in controlling labor hours and keeping the staff at a good economic staffing level.

SOME EXAMPLES OF ACCOMPLISHMENTS

In the quality control department of a large New England manufacturer, the work force of 350 inspectors was reduced by 27% for a savings of one million four hundred seventy-four thousand dollars through the implementation of a cost reduction program. The thoroughness of inspection in all areas was not changed. Where 100% inspection was used, it continued. In other areas, the statistical sampling techniques were not changed.

A midwest manufacturer of animal feeds was able to cut his shipping and warehouse operations by about 50% while achieving a better delivery performance and increasing his floor space utilization. A manufacturing company on the East Coast that was having a severe morale problem because of poor custodial operations saw a complete turnabout when the program was applied. The degree of cleanliness was improved considerably even as costs were reduced.

A New York hospital realized a cost reduction of about 30% in its ancillary functions. The reaction of the head nurse was one of surprise to discover that so much "busy" work could be accomplished. The savings were applied to enhance nursing service.

CUSTODIAL SERVICES

Cleaning services are probably among the simplest for which to develop a good program. This is true because the activities involved are routine, reasonably simple, and predictable and occur with a specific frequency.

The approach is to define all of the work that must be accomplished on a weekly, daily, or less-frequent basis. The activities are then observed to determine the specific time required to perform them. Once this has been accomplished, the activities are put into a logical step-by-step routine, which the custodian is then trained to follow. Most companies prefer that the custodian not be given anything in writing. Training consists of walking the person through the activities until he or she understands the routine.

In implementing the control, the supervisor must have continuously updated knowledge to permit him or her to check on the progress of each person. The supervisor must know that each worker is on schedule and must have an ability to check on the quality of the work. Look at Exhibit 9.1. It represents a typical custodial schedule. Note that the schedule has specific accomplishments within given time frames. In practice, the supervisor carries the schedule for each person under his or her control.

As the supervisor makes the rounds, the first thing to do is to go to the area where the custodian is *scheduled to be* at that particular time. A determination is made that the individual is or is not on schedule. If on schedule, the block is checked. If not, the reason for being off schedule is noted, corrective action taken to minimize the lost time and instructions given as to what the person doing the work must do to catch up. For example, if 20 minutes have been lost, the

SCHEDULE #15

NAME: _____   DATE: _____

PLANNED		LOC.	ACTIVITY	COM.	SUPERVISORY CHK				
START	STOP				SCHED.		QUALITY		
					ON	OFF	G	F	P
7:00		1F	Service mens washroom						
		Guard	Service mens washroom						
		1G	Service mens washroom						
		Recp.	Service mens washroom						
		1Y	Service mens washroom						
		1A	Sweep Plant Service locker rooms						
		1D	Sweep & empty rubbish Incoming Material Insp.						
	8:00	1E	Sweep 1E door to elevator						
			Sweep & empty rubbish Receiving						
8:00		1C	Sweep locker room						
			Service mens washroom						
		CX	Sweep & empty rubbish Millwrights area						
			Clean & service mens washrooms & locker room						
			Sweep & empty rubbish Paint Shop & locker room and office						
	9:00		Sweep aisle stairs under lift						
9:00	9:10		BREAK						
9:10		1D	Clean & service all drinking fountains						
	10:15		Box trucks to compactor						
10:15		1E/1D	Sweep aisle						
			Sweep Small Store						
	11:06	1F	Sweep storage						
11:06	11:42		LUNCH						
11:42		1B	Sweep aisle						
		C/G	Sweep dock						
	1:00	E/D	Relieve elevator operator						
1:00	1:10		BREAK						
1:10	3:18	3K	Empty trucks as needed						

Exhibit 9–1.

supervisor will select which 20 minutes of work will be skipped on that day or may request that the custodian work 20 minutes of overtime.

The supervisor makes appropriate notes on the schedule which, upon completion, is filed in a folder by custodian name. In this manner, a record of individual performance is maintained.

How does this system save money? Very simply. Historically, custodial jobs have been created in a loose manner without application of realistic time elements. A reorganization of the custodial routine, it will be found, can assign between 25 and 30% additional work to each custodian, and this addition will constitute a reasonable day's workload.

The application of this technique in a western university program drew comments from the custodial staff such as, "For the first time, I feel I have enough work to do and I like that." Another comment alluded to the feeling of satisfaction that a custodian got from being "visited" by the supervisor several times a day and learning that her work was satisfactory. The quality improvement is brought about by the simple fact that the custodial supervisor is in a position to check the areas immediately before the worker's current location. A determination can be made that the *just-completed* areas have been cleaned to the supervisor's satisfaction. If not, on-the-spot instruction can be given. Care must be taken that the worker is not reprimanded but instructed. This type of scheduling also provides the opportunity to give recognition to the worker for a job well done.

Tasks that must be accomplished on a less than weekly basis can be organized into a calendar schedule. The tasks are listed in a column on the left. A calendar is laid out across the top by week. Opposite each task and in the weeks in which the task is to be performed, the required hours are posted. These can easily be downfooted by week to determine the weekly load. This enables management to have full knowledge of the manpower needs. From this, two approaches (or a combination) are available.

The first approach, when the work load is heavy enough and can be balanced reasonably well on a daily basis, would be to designate specific individuals to perform periodic tasks. Daily routines can be developed or specific assignments made. The individual is "loaded" each day with activities that constitute a reasonable day's work.

The second method is to allow a certain amount of slack time in each worker's schedule. Supervision can then assign work daily from the periodic list to fill in the slack time. This has the advantage of providing the worker a daily change from the regular routine, which can be a welcome relief.

SCHEDULING SHIPPING OPERATIONS

The key to controlling the labor cost at the shipping dock is the proper assignment and supervision of the work force to coincide with the fluctuations of volume and work mix. The degree of predictability and planning that can be accomplished will play an important part in control. In some operations, communication and cooperation between the dock foreman and the traffic department are essential. Proper staging of materials must be considered along with truck or rail car schedules.

Perhaps the most complex and difficult shipping operation ever experienced by the author was in a Long Island bakery. A less complex but similar type of operation was in a bakery in Pittsburgh. Both faced the same essential problem, that is, to load a large number of route trucks and trailer trucks with fresh product on a daily basis. In each case, the major advantage of predictability was evident. The same trucks would be at the same assigned position at the same time each day. The herculean task, was to move the product from the production line to the trucks in an expeditious manner.

In the Long Island bakery, the complexity of product mix was the essential ingredient of the system that had to be controlled. This was accomplished by unloading from the production line directly onto moving racks attached to a monorail system. Each rack was then directed to a location where the product was unloaded to a staging rack. Only the amount of each product required for the staging rack would be unloaded. The racks in turn would be moved to the loading dock and the product transferred to the trucks, a three stage operation that was very labor intensive. The key cost reduction element was the redesign of the staging racks to allow them to be moved into the trucks, eliminating one complete handling of the product.

In the Pittsburgh bakery, which had a considerably smaller problem of product complexity, the product moved from the ovens through packaging to the loading dock via a continuous conveyor belt. At the truck loading end, the product had to be manually removed from the conveyor to racks that were manually moved from truck to truck. Each truck's requirement was manually unloaded from the rack. The material-handling costs were considerably reduced by the extension of the conveyors further into the loading area, which cut down on the travel requirements for the manually moved racks. Most shipping operations can become much more cost effective through the application of simple scheduling tools that permit better planning and utilization of time, space, and equipment.

A good example of controlling the activities at the shipping dock is found in the operation of a midwest producer of animal feeds. The operation was basically simple. A customer would call in the order one to two days in advance. The order would be written up and sent to the warehouse on the shipping date for picking and the pallets moved to the shipping dock.

The problem involved several items. One was limited staging space and another was that the order of arrival of the customer's racks was unpredictable. The amount of labor involved in jockeying material around to accommodate the loading of trucks as they arrived was very costly. An additional complication was the variety in the size of orders, which affected truck loading times. With dock space available for only 18 trucks at a time, the dimensions of the problem were considerable. Historically, the solution had been to apply more and more labor hours. Here is how the problem was solved and costs reduced by more than 50%, while customer service was greatly improved and truck time at the docks reduced.

First, studies were made to determine how long it took to load a pallet of product onto a truck from various points along the dock, allowing for the fact that not every truck would wind up in the exact slot designated. A reasonable time per pallet was determined. A conversion chart was established that would enable the order takers to convert an order into the time required to load a truck (see Exhibit 9.2). This data was put on the order.

The order takers were instructed to request an approximate time of arrival of the customer's truck. The orders were then sent to a "dock scheduling desk" where the truck would be scheduled at the time given and allocated an appropriate amount of dock time. In this manner, it became a simple matter not overloading the dock. As the dock became loaded to capacity for any time period, the order

CUSTOMER TRUCK SACK LOADING CONVERSION CHART

(Based on 2-man Crew)

No. of Pallets	1	2	3	4	5	6	7	8	9	10	11	12	13	14	15	16	17	18	19	20	21	22	23
33 1/3 #	5	10	14	19	23	28	32	37	41	46	50	55	59	64	68	73	77	82	86	91	95	100	104
25 #	6	12	17	23	28	34	39	45	50	56	61	67	72	78	83	89	94	100	105	111	116	122	127
50/100 #	5	10	14	18	22	26	30	34	38	42	46	50	54	58	62	66	70	74	78	82	86	90	94

Procedure:

1) Count the number of pallets on the order of a given size package.
   Note: 50- and 100-pound sacks may be counted together.

2) Look across the top line of the chart and find the number counted.

3) Immediately below the count, and opposite the size counted, find the number of minutes of loading time. Record this.

4) Continue with each size on the order.

5) Total the minutes for all sizes.

   Example: 5 pallets of 33 1/3   = 18
                10 pallets of 25   = 55
                8 pallets of 50 - & 100 -lb. = 32
                                            ────
                                        105 Minutes

6) Record 105 on the order, in the space marked "Plan Load Hours _____."

Exhibit 9–2.

takers were informed and would give alternate times to the customers as close to the requested times as possible. The scheduled arrival time of each truck was placed on the order.

Now when orders went to the warehouse for picking, they could be put in the time frame of the planned arrival of the vehicles. This provided a sequence of staging orders throughout the day on a planned basis. The problem of material staging at the dock was considerably reduced.

Finally, the dock foreman was able to benefit from the truck loading end. He could control his work assignments. Now, on arrival, each order had a time element for loading attached to it. The foreman could plan the utilization of his labor. He knew the work load in labor hours for the day, which provided his total labor requirement. He could assign his people by truck, knowing how long it would take them to load each one. In a word, he had control.

In addition, the dock foreman was able to plan the positioning of trucks as they arrived. Not all trucks arrived exactly as planned, but once in, their departure was highly predictable so he could better plan the positioning of trucks to minimize distances for movement.

This simple procedure, once installed, resulted in a surprising 60% labor reduction. Since the company planned its production runs to coincide with the 48 hour service time, additional benefits were derived for production scheduling in setting up product sequences that helped to reduce warehouse space utilization and, in many cases, avoided product runs having to occupy space in the warehouse at all.

Exhibit 9.2 illustrates how the truck scheduling and loading works. Each customer is listed on the form in the sequence of anticipated arrival. The order number and scheduled time of arrival is posted next to each customer's name. The plan load time is figured from the conversion chart (Exhibit 9.3). The actual *time in* is posted when the truck arrives at the dock. The start-time and stop-time are put in at the time of loading, with the actual *load minutes*.

By multiplying the actual load minutes by the *crew size,* the *actual man minutes* are calculated and posted. The plan load minutes multiplied by the crew size gives the *earned* minutes. If the actual exceeds the earned minutes by an extended amount, a reason for the *off schedule condition* is written in by the foreman. These two columns

TRUCK REPORT

Date _____

Customer	Order No.	Time Schld	Time In	Plan Load Mins.	Start Time	Stop Time	Actual Load Mins.	Crew Size	Earn Mins.	Act'l Man Mins.	Reason for Off-Schedule Condition
	TOTALS									÷ =	% PRODUCTIVITY

Exhibit 9-3.

can be downfooted, the earned total divided by the actual total and a productivity arrived at for the day's activity.

With this kind of planning and control, the foreman is realistically managing his operation and the time of his people.

A DIFFERENT SITUATION

A small New Jersey manufacturer that custom produces electronic devices has a production cycle of approximately six weeks. Most orders are small, from only a few pieces to a few hundred. Whole carload or truckload shipments are unheard of. The shipping foreman, who is also the traffic manager, ships by common carrier.

The foreman was quite skilled in scheduling the carriers. His problem was expensive labor costs in the shipping department, which he justified by the fact that he almost invariably had little backlog at the docks. He was encouraged to estimate the loading time for each order (or group of orders) designated for shipment by a particular carrier. He soon learned that if he added up all of his estimates for loading on any one day, his total labor requirement was about 50 to 70% of his actual labor force. When he assigned a crew to load orders based on his estimates and observed their actual performance, they performed within a few percentage points of the estimates.

He was then encouraged to allow a half day's backlog to build up at the docks so that he had more time to plan his labor utilization. With this procedure, he found that he could accomplish his shipments with an average of 36% less labor cost.

COST REDUCTION IN THE WAREHOUSE

In warehouse operations, several factors apply. Labor and space utilization can take on equal importance.

In the case of a large Kentucky distillery, the company was about to enlarge the shipping warehouse at a cost of a quarter of a million dollars because the warehouse was so continuously overloaded that material movement was a costly process. Careful investigation revealed that production was not geared properly to the finished goods shipments with resulting overloads of certain products. By recapping the daily movement of product in and out of the warehouse for a six month period, it was discovered that a change in the production cycle would reduce the inventory, creating more cube space and canceling the need for expansion.

Finished-goods warehouses must be keyed to the shipping function. Raw-material warehouses, on the other hand, must relate to the manufacturing departments. A warehouse that stores subassemblies has to be set up to facilitate the picking process for order assembly. In all cases, planning of the material movement process will result in hours of labor savings and very often will assist in reducing the space requirements.

In the case of the animal feed manufacturer mentioned earlier, we see a prime example of controlling a shipping warehouse. The warehouse foreman, who must plan the deployment of his labor force, must have knowledge of the truck schedule. This schedule was prepared by the shipping foreman on the prior day and a copy sent to the warehouse. The warehouse foreman must also have knowledge of the planned input to the warehouse for the day. Production control provides that data.

The task now is to convert the volume of product moved into and out of the warehouse into labor hours. This is done by converting the volumes into time requirements and establishing the priority of movement. The foreman, using the truck schedule and his order copies, will set up the priorities for the order-picking process.

Using the conversion chart shown as Exhibit 9.4, the foreman determines the time requirements needed to move the material to or from each *spot* or location. The number of pallets has been figured and entered on the Warehouse Schedule Control sheet (Exhibit 9.5). The time requirements are posted under the pallet number by spot. This tells him how many men he needs for each spot or location in whole numbers or fractions. He can then deploy his people, inserting their names in the *Assign To* boxes.

The totals can be figured out (lower left) as well as the available man-hours (lower right) for comparison and for ensuring that the correct number of man-hours are available. In this manner, excess hours can be utilized elsewhere or additional hours procured to ensure that the day's work will be accomplished.

The same or very similar types of planning tools will apply to most warehousing operations. The key is to develop the time requirements and then convert the work volume to manpower needs.

When developing this detail, the coordinator or person assigned will become intimately familiar with the warehouse. Special attention

MATERIAL MOVEMENT CONVERSION CHART

(Based on 1-man crew)

No. of Pallets	1	2	3	4	5	6	7	8	9	10	11	12	13	14	15	16	17	18	19	20	21	22	23
33 1/3	10	20	29	38	47	56	65	74	83	92	101	110	119	128	137	146	155	164	173	182	191	200	209
25 #	12	24	35	46	57	68	79	90	101	112	123	134	145	156	167	178	189	200	211	222	233	244	255
50/100 #	9	18	26	34	42	50	58	66	74	82	90	98	106	114	122	130	138	146	154	162	170	178	186

1. DETERMINE THE NUMBER OF PALLETS OF EACH SIZE SACK TO BE MOVED.

2. UNDER THE NUMBER AND OPPOSITE THE SACK SIZE, FIND THE PLANNED MINUTES.

Exhibit 9–4.

WAREHOUSE SCHEDULE CONTROL

Date _____

	TO SHIPPING					FROM PRODUCTION					
SPOT	1-2	2-2	3-2	4-2		1-3	2-3	3-3	4-3		
PALLETS Total											
TIME REQUIRED											
ASSIGN TO											

Total Floor Pallets   _____

Pallets Converted to   _____ Minutes

                 Total _____ Minutes

_____ Minutes

divided by 60 = _____ Hours

HOURS AVAILABLE

First Shift _____ Men @ 7.5 Hours = ____ Hours

Second Shift _____ Men @ 7.5 Hours = ____ Hours

                         Total = ____ Hours

Hours Available   _____

Hours Required   _____

+ or − Hours   _____

Exhibit 9–5.

should be paid to space utilization as related to the daily movement of material. The type of equipment being used should be examined. Is it the best for the purposes involved? The location of material in relation to its destination or to the point of input should be studied. Because the coordinator or person assigned will not necessarily have warehouse expertise, these points should be studied for the purpose of raising questions with those who do.

When in an operation such as this as much of the work is planned as is *practical* and the plan is carried out to the best of the foreman's ability, it is pleasantly surprising to see the favorable results that come about.

QUALITY–CONTROL SCHEDULING

In most quality-control (QC) organizations, work-scheduling techniques are not applied, with the result that staffing, most often, is in excess of real need. The basis for effective cost reduction is work measurement. Because of the nature of their work, most quality-control managers will resist the idea that work-scheduling techniques can be legitimately applied. It is incumbent upon the coordinator or person assigned to approach this department expecting to encounter resistance. It will be necessary to establish the work-time relationships very carefully and to be prepared to demonstrate them accurately.

A 100% inspection, particularly that accomplished at a bench or at the take-off point on a production line, is the easiest to measure because of the repetitiveness of the process. Several observations made by each of several inspectors should establish the reasonable expectations regarding performance for a given product. Once this has been accomplished, the best way to proceed is to get the manager and supervisors of the quality-control department to participate in additional observations. Get their agreement that the rate established is one which can be performed continuously without jeopardizing the product quality.

Once agreement on this issue is achieved, two additional steps should follow. One is to get historical records on hours worked by the inspectors and the quantity of product inspected for the same period of time. For a convincing sampling, a three month record should suffice. It will be necessary to convert the hours and units to pieces per hour or, reciprocally, hours per piece. Comparing this to the established R/E (reasonable expectation of performance), it will be found that actual inspections fall below the R/E by 15 to 30%. It will probably be necessary, at this point, to reexamine the R/E with QC management because they will find it difficult to accept that their people have been less than 100% productive.

The second step is to recap rejection rates to provide a means of ensuring that, all else being equal, they will not change. The inspectors will inherently fear that they will not be effective under a work measurement program that will provide a basis for comparison.

The staffing should be adjusted to the performance expectations before the program is implemented. Upon implementation, it will be found that the pressure of the production will bring about the required additional performance. This is true because the people will respond to the product movement almost automatically. The self-pacing of the past will give way to a normal workday pace.

Statistical sampling inspection becomes slightly more difficult because the number of pieces to be inspected changes with the findings of the initial sampling. The major difference in the approach is that the performance must be measured in terms of the number of rejects, which in turn increases the sample size, or may result in a 100% inspection. To control this situation, the batch size of product to the inspector must be controlled so that, on an after-the-fact count, the R/E can be applied to the batch and determination made that the performance is acceptable.

Roving inspection or variety checking throughout a department is more complex. The inspector is free to roam around the department, select samples from various machines, and make a variety of different tests. It is necessary to establish an R/E for each type of test that the inspector performs. The inspector will then have to make a record of the tests performed. A simple tally sheet with the types of tests listed down the left margin will suffice. Divide the sheet vertically into four time periods of the day, having the inspector put a tally mark next to each test performed in the proper time block. These can be converted into a utilization factor by multiplying the tallies by the R/E. In most instances, this conversion will demonstrate that the inspector is performing at about 50%. Enlarging the area in which the inspector roves will increase the number of tests. The result will be a need for fewer inspectors. Alternatively, if a given department has had a below-par quality performance, or if it can be demonstrated that quality can be improved through more frequent inspection, than that should be the goal rather than enlarging the area.

SUMMARY

In this chapter, we have applied the general principles of work planning, assignment, and follow-up to several operational areas that are normally very amenable to improvement from a cost reduction or productivity improvement standpoint. The considerable expenditure of company dollars in these areas requires that first-line supervision by given the tools and the training to manage the resources that make up this expense. Each company will find, because of its own unique make-up, that the application of the techniques described here will require specific adaptation to individual circumstances. The principles and illustrations given in this chapter should provide a sound base for *tailoring* the program to the situation.

10

Clerical Operations

This chapter will cover clerical operations in support of manufacturing as well service-oriented businesses, whose clerical processes are the life blood of their existence. Historically, in these areas, the lack of knowledge on the part of first-line supervisors of work loads and through-put capability results in a heavy loss of productivity. Workers often do not know what is expected of them and develop their own pace of work output. This, most often, results in lost productive time.

On the other hand, the paperwork volumes are not always related to the measurable output of product, and when the clerical workforce is adjusted to increases or decreases of product volume, serious imbalances can occur. For example, a Maryland manufacturing company that saw business volume declining cut back on clerical personnel at the same rate as the factory labor force. The company did not realize that the loss of product volume was the result of customers' placing smaller orders. Actually, the paperwork volume increased because there were more orders in the flow and a 12% increase in clerical activities. The resulting slowdown in order processing, material control, billing, and accounts receivable was devastating.

Even with the use of sophisticated word processors and computer-oriented operations which have greatly enhanced information flow in many organizations, clerical work scheduling and control is essential for the economy of the operation.

WHERE TO START

Look for those areas where a large number of clerical support people perform a relatively small number of activities. The order entry function in a manufacturing company from point of entry to the point of execution is a good example. Billing, accounts receivable, accounts payable, and general accounting are good areas to investigate. The fulfillment department in mail order operations, the underwriting department of an insurance company, the bookkeeping department of a bank are all examples of areas where the development of control will bring about economies.

HOW TO GET STARTED

The first thing that the assigned person must do is to understand the mission or purpose of the department. This can usually be accomplished by interviewing the manager and the supervisors of each section (if applicable). Have these people explain the overall function of the department and each of the respective subsections to gain a general overview.

Next, determine and flow-chart the major flows of work into, through, and out of the department. At the same time, learn how the department is organized to accomplish its mission. If an organization chart, down to the basic entry level position does not exist, one should be drawn. In either case, check the accuracy of the information.

The next step—which can become quite involved and must be done carefully and accurately—is to determine the activities that take place at each work station. It may be found that a group of people all perform the same activities all of the time. It is more likely that individuals will have specific jobs peculiar to their own work station. In either instance, the main thing is to capture all of the activities. Determination must be made as to whether this can be accomplished through the supervisor or through each individual. In either case the same basic method will apply.

ACTIVITY–LISTING RECORD

The central task is to use an *activity-listing record* to identify all activities and determine the means by which these activities can be

DEPARTMENT: POSITION:	ACTIVITY LISTING RECORD NAME:		
DESCRIPTION OF ACTIVITY TO BE PERFORMED	FREQ. CODE	UNIT	R/E

FREQUENCY CODES: A- Daily B- Weekly C- Monthly D- Quarterly E- Semi-annual F- Annual G- On demand or by occurrence

Exhibit 10-1.

quantified. Each employee, in the case of individual positions, or the supervisor, in the case of multiple positions, will fill out the form. It is best to prepare written instructions to accompany the form. The person assigned to the department should be in a position to check with each person that has been given a form, on a daily basis, to ensure his or her understanding and compliance. It should be planned that the form will be in each person's hands for a period of a week.

Exhibit 10.1 is a typical activity listings record. The person or supervisor is instructed to fill out the heading by listing each activity that is performed, starting with the daily activities and proceeding to less frequent ones. When an activity is listed, the frequency code is shown in the block next to it and corresponds to the code explanations in the right-hand margin. The columns headed "Unit" and "R/E" are not to be used. They will be used by the assigned person in his evaluation process.

DEVELOPING THE UNIT OF MEASURE

The "unit" column on the record will be filled in by the assigned person and represents that unit by which the activity will be measured and for which the R/E or reasonable expectation of performance will be developed. The proper development of the unit of measure is very important. It should represent the *most common denominator* that can legitimately be applied to the activity. It will be something tangible, that is, can be counted or measured in an easy manner.

For example: An activity is listed as "answering the telephone." The unit of measure would be the phone call. All units are not that simple. An activity listed as "typing letters" could be measured by the letter provided that all letters are of the same relative size. It is more likely that letters will vary in size. If we were to go to the least common denominator, it would necessitate counting words or even key strokes, an obviously impractical task. It is probable that the unit should be pages or perhaps half pages. It would be relatively simple to attach a time element or reasonable expectation to either and both are simple to count.

The unit of measure is best developed by observing the activity and discussing it with the person who does the work. The application of a modicum of common sense, with the thought in mind that the unit should be readily measurable in terms of time on a constant basis and easily counted, will, in most instances result in the choice of an acceptable unit.

Here are some more examples: Filing activities can be measured by the number of pieces to be filed. However, counting pieces of paper filed can be cumbersome. It can be determined that there are *x* number of pieces to be filed in an inch. It is easier to measure the pile in inches than to count pieces. The accuracy is only dependent upon the *reasonable* consistency of the number of pieces per inch. The time element to file an inch of pieces can be determined with a reasonable degree of accuracy. Mail sorting can be measured more readily by weight than by counting pieces. Within a *reasonable* degree of accuracy, volume can be calculated and a time element applied to a unit of weight. It will be found that the vast majority of clerical type functions can be readily identified in simple, measurable units.

ESTABLISHING THE R/E

The R/E is defined as the rate of performance that can be *r*easonably *e*xpected from a worker when doing his or her job under normal conditions. The rate is the time it takes to complete one unit of work. However, it can be expressed in time per unit, units per minute, or units per hour. In developing the time elements, the assigned person, very often with the assistance of the manager or supervisor, will want to observe the work in progress. It must be recognized that the R/E need not be established with stop watch accuracy. Indeed, the use of a stop watch is undesirable. With the aid of the activity listing record on which the unit of measure for each activity has been recorded, the process of determining time per unit can be established. There are a number of techniques that can be used, any one of which is acceptable, depending upon the nature of the work.

The first is by direct observation of the person doing the work. The person is first asked to demonstrate how the activity is performed and assures the observer that the activity is complete. The person is then asked to perform the activity in a normal manner for a relatively short period of time. The start and stop times are noted, and the number of units completed is recorded. This can be done several times. Varying the length of times of the observations will lead to a more accurate determination.

Another method is to have the supervisor assign a given number of units and have the person perform the function under remote observation. The observer must be able to determine that no unusual delays occur to distort the time element. Several assignments with varying volumes can be used. The start and stop times are recorded and the time per unit calculated.

Either of the above techniques should be applied to all daily activities and those less-frequent activities with varying volumes of a significant nature. The R/E established for each activity is recorded on the activity listing record. On less-frequent or small-volume activities, an estimate by the supervisor and/or the position incumbent can be used.

Some activities, even daily activities, will be found to occur regularly with the same volume or will always take the same length of time. These can be simplified by changing the unit from a volume count to an "occurrence." For example, assigning a clerk to help open mail from 8:00 to 8:30 every morning need not be measured in terms of the mail count. The activity would be listed as "assist mail room," the frequency would be "A" for daily, the unit would be "occurrence," and the R/E is listed as a half hour.

SECURING VOLUME INFORMATION

When the activity is directly related to a unit for which volume records are kept, the volume information can be obtained from the historical data. However, if the records are kept for a different time frame than desired, then the procedure that follows should apply. For example, if an item such as the number of purchase orders typed were recorded monthly and a daily or weekly volume were required, it would be necessary to get the volume on a daily/weekly basis.

The procedure is simple, but the task is tedious and should be carried out for as brief a period as is practical, usually no longer than a month. Each person records all of his activity volumes on a daily basis and summarizes them weekly, using a slash tally form.

DEPARTMENT:
POSITION:
NAME:

VARIABLE WORK VOLUME SURVEY

WEEKENDING DATE:

ACTIVITY DESCRIPTION	UNIT COUNT	MON	TUES.	WED.	THURS.	FRI.	TOTAL
PROCESS CUSTOMER ORDERS	ORDER	||||| 1	||||	|||| 111	|||| 11	||||	30
PROCESS CHANGE ORDERS	ORDER	111	11	111	1	11	11
PROCESS PTV ORDERS	ORDER	111	||||	11	11	11	14
CALL BRANCH REPRESENTATIVES	CALL	|||| |||| 11	|||| 11	||||	|||| |||| 1111	||||	42
MATCH RECEIVING TICKETS WITH INVOICES	TICKET	|||| |||| 111	|||| 111 |||| |||| ||||	|||| ||||	|||| |||| ||||	|||| 111	91
TYPE LETTERS AND MEMOS	PAGE	|||| 11	|||| 1	|||| 1	|||| 11	|||| 1111	34
TYPE TRANSMITALS	TRANS.	|||| |||| ||||	|||| |||| 1	|||| |||| 11	|||| |||| 111	|||| |||| 111	87
MAKE WEEKLY STATUS REPORT	REPORT			1			1
CHECK PERSONNEL TIME SHEETS	OCCASION					1	1
HOURS WORKED		7.5	7.5	7.5	7.5	7.5	37.5

WORK DAYS

Exhibit 10-2.

Exhibit 10.2 demonstrates the form, the information for which has come from the activity listing forms.

Each person uses one tally form per week, listing the department, position, name, and week-ending date. The form lists the activities down the left and the days of the week across the top. The person is instructed to count the units of measure as shown on the form and make a tally each time the activity is performed. These will be totaled daily and/or weekly as required. The illustration provides several examples of activities with a variety of units of measure.

The form also contains daily and weekly blocks that are not labeled. These will serve to record the time involved when multiplying the volume tally totals by the R/E. The R/E is not listed on the form but is shown on the activity listing record. The person doing the summarizing will cross-reference to the activity listing record when doing this summary. The R/Es are inserted manually in the blank space next to the unit. In this example the R/E is expressed in minutes per unit. The end result is a reasonably accurate record of the amount of time that each incumbent actually spends accomplishing productive work. The incumbent inserts the actual hours worked each day at the location and totals the tallies weekly. It is not unusual to find that out of the total of work week hours available, the incumbent will be productive only a small percentage of the time. Care must be taken to ensure that people are not criticized for this. It is not the fault of the person but the failure of management to construct each position as a reasonably full-time job. The eventual development of the work controls will produce a more productive workforce, trimmed to the realistic needs of the department.

During the period that the tallies are being recorded, the person assigned, and/or the supervisor can be busy establishing the R/Es as previously described.

LOADING THE POSITION

In Exhibit 10.3, the person assigned has inserted the R/Es (in minutes) for each activity, multiplied the tallies by the R/E and inserted the real time in the small block for each day and for the week. He has converted the minutes to hours for comparison against the hours worked. It becomes evident that the job is loaded to only 53% of its capacity. This can be accomplished for each position in the depart-

DEPARTMENT:
POSITION:
NAME:

WEEKENDING DATE:

VARIABLE WORK VOLUME SURVEY

ACTIVITY DESCRIPTION	UNIT COUNT		MON	TUES.	WED.	THURS.	FRI.	TOTAL
PROCESS CUSTOMER ORDERS	ORDER	5	30	20	40	35	25	30 / 150
PROCESS CHANGE ORDERS	ORDER	7	21	14	21	7	14	11 / 77
PROCESS PTV ORDERS	ORDER	9	27	45	18	18	18	14 / 126
CALL BRANCH REPRESENTATIVES	CALL	3	36	21	12	42	15	42 / 126
MATCH RECEIVING TICKETS WITH INVOICES	TICKET	0.5	9	15	5	13	4	91 / 46
TYPE LETTERS AND MEMOS	HALF PAGE	12	84	72	72	84	96	34 / 408
TYPE TRANSMITTALS	TRANS.	2	36	32	34	36	36	87 / 174
MAKE WEEKLY STATUS REPORT	REPORT	76			76		1	1 / 76
CHECK PERSONNEL TIME SHEETS	OCCAS-ION	15					15	1 / 15
								1198
			243	219	278	235	223	20
			4.05	3.65	4.63	3.9	3.7	
HOURS WORKED			7.5	7.5	7.5	7.5	7.5	37.5

WORK DAYS

Exhibit 10-3.

ment. Over a three to four week period, a picture develops that presents an accurate representation of the actual time requirements to accomplish the work of the department.

LOADING THE DEPARTMENT

Each position in the department can be compared against all others and a total drawn. Assuming a 15 person department, the work load could conceivably look like this:

1. Time available at 37.5 hours =   562.5
2. Average weekly hours from volume sheets   354.5
3. Gross excess hours in department   208.0
4. Full-time equivalents (208 ÷ 37.5)   5.5

From these figures another calculation should be made. The average weekly hours from the volume tallies represent a 100% performance based on the R/Es. An allowance must made for performances of less than 100% plus an allowance for absences. The normal allowance for performance would be at 85%. A calculation can be made from the personnel records for absence. Let us allow 3% for illustration purposes. Another calculation is made:

1. 562.5 hours − 3% = 545.4 hours available
2. 354.5 hours ÷ 85% = 417.0 required hours
3. Net difference = 128.4 excess hours
4. Full-time equivalents = 3.4

The figures show that three full-time positions out of fifteen can be eliminated from the department.

HOW TO REORGANIZE

In the planning stages of reorganization, the goal is to select 3 positions and distribute the work load among the remaining 12. This can be accomplished by use of the volume tally reports. Select the 3 positions that show the lowest work load. Assuming that the sheets were run for four weeks, take a weekly average of the hours of each activity for the four week period for each position. Starting with that position with the lowest total hours of work, begin, on paper, to transfer the activities and the hours to the other 12 positions.

As each activity and its related hours are transferred, a new total is drawn for the position(s) to which the activity is moved. Each of the 12 positions can be loaded to 32 hours (85% of capacity). This continues until the 3 positions are, on paper, eliminated. The work load is distributed as equitably as possible with every effort being made to balance the load among the 12.

The next step is to assure that the incumbent in each position will be able to perform the work. Some training may be required to ensure that strange or complex work loads are not dumped on a position, causing immediate chaos.

The technique, up to this point, has been to plan the operation of the department with the correct economic staffing level. The next step is to design the methods by which management and supervision can control work output and time. Without this latter step, the reductions, if made, could result in serious problems. Recognize that the work load of the remaining people will increase. They will absorb this work load only if supervision improves the planning and assigning of work. There are a variety of techniques to accomplish this.

BATCH AND ASSIGN

Many types of clerical activities lend themselves to being counted, batched, measured in terms of time, and assigned in increments of one to several hours of work. The supervisor or an assigned clerk does the counting and batching. This can work particularly well in a situation where the work flows through a series of steps to be accomplished by several groups of people.

In the order entry flow of a medium-sized New York manufacturer of duplicating machines, the order entry department consisted of a flow involving editing, pricing, taxing, typing, and distribution. Each of the five functions involved more than one clerk. As orders were received, the supervisor, with the assistance of a clerk, prepared the batches. A time element or R/E had been developed for each function. The batch ticket is shown in Exhibit 10.4. Each batch is made to provide an editor with approximately one hour's work. This regulates the size of the batches. The time element at the subsequent work stations will vary because the R/E is different for each.

The supervisor maintains control of the flow by means of a series of five "in baskets," one for each work station. Priority order is

Date		Batch # _____
Edit	_____	_____
Price	_____	_____
Tax	_____	_____
Type	_____	_____
Distribute	_____	_____

	Start	Stop
Edit	_____	_____
Price	_____	_____
Tax	_____	_____
Type	_____	_____
Distribute		

Exhibit 10–4.

controlled by numbering the batch tickets in sequence each day. The work is assigned from each basket and returned to the basket for the subsequent step. The supervisor writes in the start time at time of assignment and the stop time when completed. This can be readily compared to the time element at the top and "off schedule" conditions immediately recognized.

This type of control has several advantages. It enables supervision to maintain a balanced line. In the example given, note that the one hour at the editing station will provide only a half hour's work at the price station. Thus, it becomes evident that the ratio of price clerks to editors is one to two. The same principle applies to the other work stations. The distribution function, being the fastest would require only one person for every four editors. By cross-training people in the various functions, they can be moved to the different stations, as needed, to maintain the balance.

Another advantage to the control is that it provides for horizontal, rather than vertical, movement of work. Work will not pile up at any given station and the flow moves smoothly. By collecting the work tickets daily, the actual lapsed time of a batch can be calculated and control maintained over the total time in process.

FREE-FLOW CONTROL

In a good number of clerical functions, the supervisor does not have the opportunity to receive and assign the work. The work often comes in through the office mail directly to the worker. A telephone call can trigger a work function. A particular position can have a large variety of small functions that make it impractical to batch and assign. These are referred to as free-flow activities.

The solution here is to know how much work each person must accomplish and to be able to recognize any buildup of burdensome backlogs. The type of control is illustrated by the experience in the home office central order department of an Alabama-based wood products company.

After recording all of the activities and volumes of the myriad of activities involved and establishing R/Es for all of them, department personnel were able to reorganize and redistribute the work loads. Because of the free-flow nature of the work, a means had to be developed to keep track of the work load and to recognize the productivity of the various positions. The solution was to relate all of the work to one key volume indicator.

KEY VOLUME INDICATOR

This is a particular item that can readily be counted but that does not actually trigger each work activity. However, with enough data, a determination can be made of the time relationship between all of the work at a given work station and the particular item. Using the *variable work volume survey* (Exhibit 10.3) at each work station, workers were able to determine the actual work requirements for the various positions. The total hours were posted daily and summarized weekly on a spread sheet as shown in Exhibit 10.5. In fact, eight weeks' worth of volume tallies were used. The illustration is a shortened version.

Each position in the department has been listed in the left-hand margin. The required time per day and per week, from the daily and

REQUIRED HOURS PER DAY/WEEK FROM WORK VOLUME SURVEYS

POSITION	M	T	W	T	F	TOT	M	T	W	T	F	TOT	M	T	W	T	F	TOT	M	T	W	T	F	TOT
MILL SCHEDULER	3.2	3.4	2.8	3.2	3.5	16.1	3.3	3.5	2.4	3.3	3.6	16.6	3.0	3.2	2.6	3.0	3.3	15.1	3.4	3.6	3.0	3.4	3.7	17.1
MILL SCHEDULER	2.8	3.0	2.6	3.0	3.0	14.2	2.4	2.9	3.1	2.7	3.1	14.7	2.6	2.8	2.9	2.4	2.8	13.2	2.8	3.0	3.2	2.8	3.2	15.2
ASS'T SCHEDULER	3.9	3.6	3.3	4.0	4.0	18.0	4.3	3.7	3.4	4.1	4.1	19.5	3.7	4.0	3.4	3.1	3.8	18.0	4.1	4.4	3.8	3.5	4.2	20.0
CLERK TYPIST	2.5	2.6	2.3	2.6	—	12.6	2.6	2.7	2.6	3.0	—	13.1	1.9	2.4	2.4	2.3	2.7	11.5	2.3	2.6	2.8	2.7	3.1	13.5
FILE CLERK	3.9	4.2	3.8	4.0	4.0	19.6	3.8	4.0	4.3	3.4	4.1	20.1	3.5	3.7	4.0	3.6	3.8	18.6	3.4	4.1	4.4	4.0	4.2	20.6
COMMODITY CLERK	5.6	5.4	5.2	5.2	5.6	27.0	5.3	5.7	5.5	5.3	5.7	27.5	5.0	5.4	5.5	5.0	5.1	26.0	5.6	5.8	5.6	5.4	5.8	28.0
ORDERS PROCESSED	10	12	11	13	12	58	11	11	10	12	12	56	11	10	12	12	9	54	12	13	12	11	12	60
MILL SCHEDULER	.32	.29	.23	.27	.27	.27	.30	.32	.29	.23	.31	.30	.33	.31	.23	.23	.31	.28	.28	.28	.23	.30	.31	.29
MILL SCHEDULER	.24	.23	.24	.23	.23	.24	.26	.26	.31	.23	.26	.26	.24	.29	.29	.23	.24	.27	.31	.23	.27	.24	.27	.25
ASS'T SCHEDULER	.34	.33	.30	.30	.32	.32	.36	.34	.37	.28	.34	.35	.34	.41	.33	.31	.32	.33	.31	.31	.32	.31	.35	.33
CLERK TYPIST	.21	.21	.23	.22	.23	.22	.20	.23	.17	.22	.23	.23	.18	.21	.18	.42	.23	.21	.19	.20	.23	.23	.26	.23
FILE CLERK	.37	.33	.35	.35	.31	.34	.35	.36	.43	.33	.34	.36	.39	.31	.36	.36	.42	.34	.33	.32	.36	.36	.35	.34
COMMODITY CLERK	.52	.46	.43	.44	.43	.47	.48	.52	.55	.44	.48	.49	.56	.45	.45	.47	.48	.48	.45	.46	.47	.44	.48	.47

HOURS PER ORDER

MILL SCHEDULER	.30
MILL SCHEDULER	.25
ASS'T SCHEDULER	.34
CLERK TYPIST	.23
FILE CLERK	.34
COMMODITY CLERK	.48

Exhibit 10-5.

weekly bottom line of the work volume survey, has been entered. The selected key volume indicator is "orders processed." This is shown in the left-hand margin and the daily/weekly volumes for the same days and weeks has been entered.

By dividing the required hours each day by the volume of orders processed, the required hours per order processed is determined. The same is done with the weekly totals. Look first at the four weekly total hours per order processed.

Mill scheduler	.27	.30	.30	.29
Mill scheduler	.24	.26	.24	.25
Ass't scheduler	.32	.35	.33	.33
Clerk typist	.22	.23	.21	.23
File clerk	.34	.36	.34	.34
Commodity clerk	.47	.49	.48	.47

Select the highest hours per order processed and compare this figure to the daily figures. For example, the first mill scheduler's highest is .30. On the daily computations, the lowest is .23 and the highest is .33. The differences from .30 are .07 on the low side and .03 on the high, a relatively insignificant difference for the purpose. Some judgement is involved, but for all practical purposes an R/E for each position, based on the number of orders, can be established. These are shown at the bottom of the exhibit. Note that not all have been set up at the high point. Differences from high to low and in the frequency of occurrences are part of the judgemental considerations.

The R/E can now be applied to the order volume and determination made as to the work load for each station or position. In this manner, the supervisor has a constant picture of the load and can shift work loads to achieve balance. The final determination of the staffing for this group was made by applying the R/E per order to the highest monthly volume of the most recent 12 months. This is what it showed:

Order volume for March = 273 (21 working days)
Order volume per day = 13 × 5 = 65 per week

		Hr. Req.	Hr. Avail.	Surplus
Mill scheduler at	.30	19.50	37.5	+18
Mill scheduler at	.25	16.25	37.5	+21.5
Assist scheduler	.34	22.10	37.5	+15.4
Clerk typist at	.23	14.95	37.5	+22.5
File clerk at	.34	22.10	37.5	+15.4
Commodity clerk at	.48	31.20	37.5	+ 6.3

With this information the group was reorganized. The position of assistant scheduler was eliminated and the work absorbed by the two mill schedulers. The file clerk's position was eliminated with most of the work absorbed by the typist and a small amount by the commodity clerk, and several activities were passed up the line to the schedulers.

SUMMARY

Though clerical operations often present problems because of complexity and variable volumes, the same basic principles are involved in their development and control. Self-pacing by the work force results in lost time and is a detriment to service. The principles outlined in this chapter will give supervision the ability to establish and maintain the pace of the work force. As long as this pace is reasonable, the results will be surprisingly good, not only from an economic standpoint but also from the point of view of morale.

11

Reducing Costs and Improving Performance in Engineering Services

Engineering departments can benefit greatly from the type of work scheduling that brings about cost reductions in other departments. Though most engineering departments work under deadlines, particularly those involved in project-type work, it will be found that each individual engineer controls his own time. It is often said that an engineer will complete 90% of his work in the last 10% of his allocated time. This is, no doubt, an exaggeration. However, the lack of finely tuned planning and short-range follow-up results in a heavy loss of productive capacity. This chapter will cover proven methods of recovering much of this productive capacity, resulting in as much as a 30% increase in work output. Even in sophisticated departments that employ Pert or CPM techniques, the methods described here will improve the ability of the group to better forecast manpower requirements, improve service, and reduce costs.

STARTING AT THE FRONT END

Requests for services will normally arrive from a variety of departments within the organization. The first thing that must be accomplished is to analyze each incoming request and determine the requirements necessary to schedule and control it. To this end, a log is established to record all incoming requests. Designed to ensure that the analytical step is taken, the log contains information that can only be inserted as the result of the initial analysis.

Exhibit 11.1 is an example of such a log. It was developed for the

WEEKLY INPUT & COMPLETION LOG
INTERNAL & EXTERNAL REQUESTS

W/E: _____
DEPT: _____
MGR: _____

I.D. #	PROJ. #	REQUEST BY & DATE	DESCRIPTION OF PROJECT	ASSIGNED TO	ESTIMATED		ACTUAL	
					MAN HRS	DATE COMP.	MAN HRS	DATE COMP.

Exhibit 11-1.

145

engineering department of a southwestern plant of one of the country's largest electrical products manufacturing companies. The company had an unprecedented work load because of new product development. Hiring additional engineers would not meet the deadlines imposed by the marketplace. Something else had to be done immediately. Adopting the format of the log in Exhibit 11.1 was the initial step.

Each incoming request was given an identification number corresponding to the project involved.These were recorded as received with the requestor's name and the date received. A brief description of the project was inserted. To comply with the requirement of the log to insert the estimated man-hours and planned completion date (and, later, the actual man-hours and actual completion date) it was necessary to analyze the request in some depth. This established the requirement of analyzing the request as an initial step. The person assigned was filled in later.

ANALYSIS OF REQUESTS FOR SERVICE

This procedure can be as simple as looking at the request document and estimating that it will take from one to a few hours of a specific engineering expertise, or as difficult as an in-depth determination of man-hours for a complex, long-term project. The former only requires that the few hours be recorded on the request format and entered in the log, whereas the latter can involve several hours of analysis before an estimate is arrived at. The larger the job, the more detailed the analysis must be. The objective is to reduce the job or project to logical segments of controllable man-hours. The responsibility for accomplishing this goal rests with engineering management.

The upper portion of the form (Exhibit 11.2) is designed for identification purposes. The remaining part is for a breakdown of the project into logical phases. A logical phase may be determined in various ways. A phase can be a point at which the results *require* review before proceeding. It can also be a point at which the project development requires the transition to, or introduction of, a different engineering talent. Another definition of a phase could be a breakpoint in time to review the status. Engineering management must exercise judgement in phasing the project, keeping in mind the

		STANDARD REQUEST CONTROL		DEPT: _____ MGR: _____ DATE _____			

I.D. # _____ PROJ. # _____			EST. HRS. _____ ACT. HRS. _____		
REQUESTOR'S NAME _____			EST. DATE _____ ACT. DATE _____		
COMPANY _____					

PROJECT DESCRIPTION

PHASE	ASSIGN TO	DATE ASSIGN / DUE	PROJECT PHASE	HOURS REQUIRED			
				SUPV.		ENG.	
				PL	ACT	PL	ACT
1							
2							
3							
4							
5							
6							
			SUB-TOTAL				

Exhibit 11–2.

need to meet deadlines. It is conceivable that more than one phase can be ongoing simultaneously or that phases can overlap in time.

Each phase is written in under "Project Phase." The estimate of hours to be applied to each phase, where applicable, is divided between supervisory time and engineering time. When a particular phase involves a specific talent from the group (such as drafting), the appropriate supervisor should be involved in the estimating process.

Once the phases have been estimated, they are totaled to establish the man-hours required to produce the project. The next step is to examine the deadline requirements and determine that sufficient man-hours can be mustered to permit completion by that deadline in the proper sequence. This introduces an additional element of planning. To muster the necessary talent, the work-load assignments of all members of the department must be tracked.

INDIVIDUAL WORK LOAD ASSIGNMENTS

As each individual is assigned to a project or several projects, his or her time becomes committed. If the department is to be properly loaded, then each engineer's time must be tracked. This is accomplished on a weekly calendar schedule such as is shown in Exhibit 11.3.

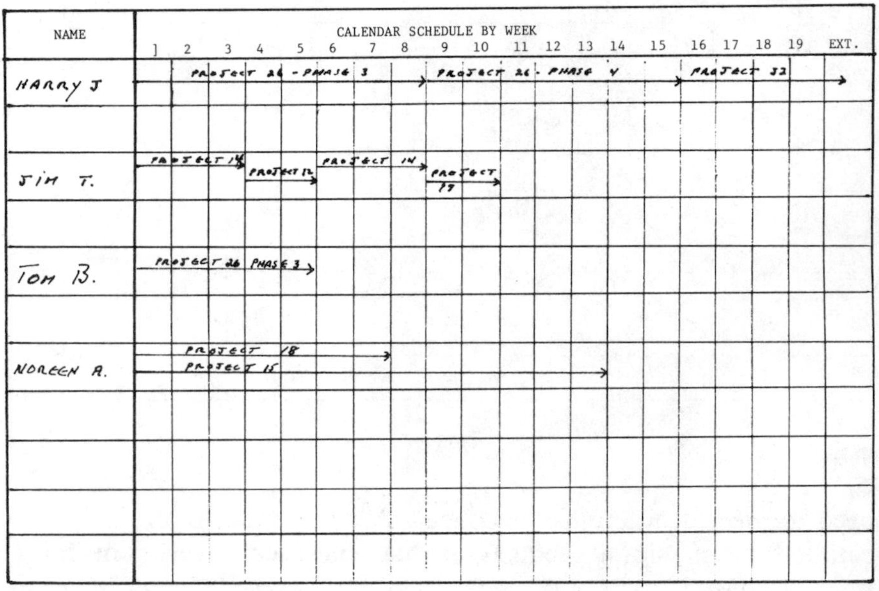

Exhibit 11-3.

As each project, phase, or other work assignment is made, the engineer's hours are committed to it and plotted against his name. By simply drawing an arrow through the fully committed weeks (37.5 hours is normal) and, as necessary, into a non-fully committed week, it can be recognized at a glance when any engineer will become availabe for additional work. Some engineers may be scheduled for more than one project, working on them either alternatively or simultaneously. The schedule format can be drawn out to the number of weeks desired. In the exhibit, with a 19 week period, the final column is designed to show that a particular engineer is scheduled beyond the format period and will be picked up on another sheet.

In the exhibit, Harry J. is scheduled with back-to-back assignments extending beyond 19 weeks. Jim T. has been assigned project 14 for three weeks, at the end of which time he will have a hiatus and will spend two weeks on project 12, go back to 14 for three weeks and then to project 17. The schedule shows him available starting in week 11.

Tom B. is involved in one project and is available for assignment in week 6. His work is part of project 26, phase 3, the same being worked on by Harry J. Noreen A. is spending approximately 50% of her time on project 18 and 50% on project 15. She will be available for assignment in week 8 (50%) or can be reassigned to work full time on project 15, which will shorten the project's time span.

THE NEED TO DETERMINE THE BACKLOG

At the outset of the scheduling procedures, the work in process or backlog hours must be determined for each engineer so that the bar chart accurately reflects the current position of everyone in the department. New work can then be added or can displace current assignments as priorities demand.

DEVELOPING CONTROL

Up to this point, the preliminary requirements have been satisfied, that is, all incoming work is estimated in terms of time; when required, projects are phase estimated; each project is then logged in to the department; the current work load of each member is known. New work can now be scheduled in the department.

Once this has been accomplished, supervision must be put in the position of being able to monitor progress, determine that work is or is not proceeding as scheduled and take corrective action as required. Recognize that all of the time elements are estimated. They should have been intelligently estimated, but estimating is not an exact science.

The method to be used by the supervisor is a weekly review of the accomplishments of the prior week and an agreement with the engineer on the goals for the coming week.

ESTABLISHING GOALS

The supervisor will have the closest direct knowledge of all of his or her assigned projects and/or phases of projects. He or she will have knowledge of the project schedules as well as the requirements. The task, then is to reduce the immediate assignment (part of project or phase) to a requirement that the work be accomplished within a relatively short time frame, namely, a one week period.

Goals are established for each coming week by means of a weekly plan worked out with the engineer. The plan is reduced to writing and consists merely of listing the things that both agree must be accomplished in the coming week. The project description is the source document or the project phase. Each item that must be accomplished is estimated in terms of time. The time elements are a portion of the project or phase. The hours for each engineer must not exceed normal working hours unless overtime is authorized.

Exhibit 11.4 is a simple illustration of the type of format that can be used to enable the engineer to keep track of his own accomplishments as the week progresses. The descriptive language should be kept to a meaningful minimum. The engineer and the supervisor should each retain a copy.

CHECKING THE RESULTS

At intervals of one week or more, the supervisor and the engineer review results. The review can be more frequent, at the discretion of either, particularly if events occur that interrupt the engineer's progress on the assignment. It is the engineer's responsibility to keep track of the actual hours spent on each item and the percentage of the job

Engineering Weekly Assignment Schedule

Project Number: _____   Phase Number: _____   Assigned To: _____

1) Item Description: _____

_____

_____

_____

_____

_____

   Hours Planned: _____   Actual Hours Spent: _____
   % Completed: MON ____ TUE ____ WED ____ THUR ____ FRI ____

2) Item Description: _____

_____

_____

_____

_____

_____

   Hours Planned: _____   Actual Hours Spent: _____
   % Completed: MON ____ TUE ____ WED ____ THUR ____ FRI ____

3) Item Description: _____

_____

_____

_____

_____

_____

   Hours Planned: _____   Actual Hours Spent: _____
   % Completed: MON ____ TUE ____ WED ____ THUR ____ FRI ____

Exhibit 11–4.

completed by day of the week. He is always in a position of knowing where he stands relative to the assignment.

During the same meeting that the plan for the coming week is made, the actual results of the prior week are reviewed. If any items are incomplete, they will be carried over to the coming week's plan. The supervisor will require an explanation of incomplete items and of completed items on which too many hours were spent.

RECORDING THE RESULTS

The supervisor has the responsibility for updating the work-load assignment sheets; the results of each individual record of accomplishment reflect a deviation that will either extend or contract the assignment. He accomplishes this initially through his review of the weekly assignment schedule. If all work was accomplished within the estimated time frame, the schedule sheet itself can be filed. The work-load record requires no updating as long as it is on schedule.

However, many things can happen that cause the assigned work to remain incomplete or that absorb more than the planned hours. During the review with the engineer, the supervisor makes out a variance report on exceptions that are serious enough to affect the work load. Such things as absenteeism, the introduction of unforeseen circumstances, and outside interferences can all play a part in causing the schedule to be incomplete.

Recognize that the actual hours recorded must be fed back to the standard request control and to the weekly input and completion log. As these hours are reviewed in total and are found to be in excess of the plan, management will certainly become aware. If plan due dates are missed, an explanation will be in order. It is incumbent upon the supervisor to minimize excess hours and missed due dates. His best tool for recognizing and reporting these problems as they happen is the same tool that brings them to his attention, namely, the weekly variance report.

WEEKLY VARIANCE REPORT

The *weekly variance report* can take one or two forms. It can be either an individual report for each variance, directed to the person responsible for keeping the departmental records updated, or it can be a single report on which each of the variances experienced by the supervisor's people is recorded as a line item. The information reported is the same for the variances experienced.

Exhibit 11.5 is an example of a line item variance report. Its first function is to record discrepancies that may or will have an impact

WEEKLY VARIANCE REPORT

SUPERVISOR: _____   SECTION: _____   W.E. DATE: _____

PROJ. ID AND PHASE NO.	PLAN HRS	ACT HRS	+ OR − DIFF	REASON FOR VARIANCE AND CORRECTIVE ACTION	DUE DATE AFFECTED ?

Exhibit 11–5.

on the number of actual hours used compared to the plan hours. This item will certainly affect the cost of the project. The second function is to record any slippage that may or will affect the due date of the project or phase. This is particularly important when the delay will affect other phases of a project or when a due date is extremely critical.

As mentioned earlier, the information on the weekly variance report is fed back to the standard request control and the weekly input and completion log. It is equally important that the supervisor and the engineer be continuously alerted to the schedule condition and manpower expenditures on a short-term basis. Adjustments made on a short-term basis are much more manageable than those required after a longer-range slippage has caused havoc.

The report also gives the supervisor an opportunity to demonstrate to management that he is in control, is taking appropriate corrective action, and is directly managing his projects and his people.

DEPARTMENTAL BACKLOG CONTROL

It is important that management be kept aware of the backlog in the department. Only in this manner can continuous evaluations be made of the manpower requirements. The more sectionalized the department, the more important the backlog data. Each supervisor must contribute his data so that a summary for the department can be made.

Exhibit 11.6 shows a typical backlog report to be filled out by a supervisor. The report is designed to fit the work into specific ranges so that both short- and long-term projects can be distinguished.

The major judgement factor is estimating the completed hours of work still in progress. The best approach is to use a percentage factor of the original estimate. A record must be kept of the hours reported

WEEKLY BACKLOG REPORT

REQUEST RANGE (WEEKS)	0 – 5		6 – 10		11 – 15		15 +	
	NO	HRS	NO	HRS	NO	HRS	NO	HRS
BEGINNING BACKLOG								
INCOMING REQUESTS								
TOTAL								
COMPLETED REQUESTS								
BACKLOG								
COMPLETED HOURS ON JOBS IN PROGRESS	✕		✕		✕		✕	
NET BACKLOG								

BEGINNING BACKLOG.	Enter the number of jobs and hours from prior week's NET BACKLOG.
INCOMING REQUESTS.	Enter the number of jobs and estimated hours received during the week.
TOTAL.	Total of above.
COMPLETED REQUESTS.	1) Enter the number of requests that have been completed.
	2) Enter the number of estimated hours that remained on that request since last deletion of hours previously reported as COMPLETED HOURS ON JOBS IN PROGRESS.
BACKLOG.	TOTAL minus COMPLETED REQUESTS
COMPLETED HOURS ON JOBS IN PROGRESS.	Enter the estimated hours completed this week on jobs still in progress.
NET BACKLOG.	1) Same as BACKLOG number.
	2) Subtract COMPLETED HOURS ON JOBS IN PROGRESS from BACKLOG.

NOTE: Requests are entered in the appropriate range (entry date to requested or planned completion date) and remain in that range until completed.

Exhibit 11-6.

to avoid deleting more than the estimated hours without revising and adding additional estimated hours. Note that all of the hours used are estimated hours.

ESTIMATED VERSUS ACTUAL HOURS

As information is fed back to the standard request control and/or the weekly input and completion log, a percentage of estimated versus actual hours can be figured on a historical basis and can be used to calculate the actual hours required to complete the net backlog.

For example, if you have 100 net backlog hours and are running at 85% of actual performance in estimating, divide the net backlog by 85% and you will see that you need 117.6 actual hours to complete the backlog. If you are running at 115% performance you will require only 87 actual hours to complete the 100 hour backlog.

SUMMARY

The procedures as outlined in this chapter will greatly enhance the productive output of the engineering group. An improvement of 30–35% is not unusual. Target dates will be met or even improved upon in most circumstances. When the condition of the work load, compared to the availability of engineering hours, is known, the economic staffing level of the department can be maintained. The "fail safe" manner of staffing can be reduced to realistic numbers. The ability to forecast manpower requirements for future work is greatly enhanced.

Continuous follow-up on the part of engineering management will ensure that the department functions within sound economic boundaries and still is in a position to service the company's requirements.

12

Integrating the Program

Once the cost reduction/profit improvement program has begun to take shape, consideration must be given to integrating it into the company philosophy. This philosophy normally takes on a particular character that reflects the thinking of the company's top echelon, very often, indeed, the thinking of the top man.

Should the program incorporate a hardline attitude of squeezing out every bit of potential savings? How much tolerance can be allowed? What is the thinking about employee morale? Supervisor morale? Is it hardline? The very astute president of an eastern electical device company once said, "I'd rather sacrifice a few percentage points of productivity and have a happy shop." Still another prominent executive honestly believed that the best morale booster was a constant striving for achievement. Both are quite successful in their respective firms. Both achieved excellent results.

This chapter will be more technical than philosophic, but the reader must keep in mind that attitudes at the top will have a definite effect on the manner in which the program progresses. They will influence not the facts, but the presentation of the facts in the reporting system.

PYRAMIDING THE REPORTS

As previously mentioned, too many companies are thoroughly committed to after-the-fact reporting, a type of reporting that has its value as historic data but too often does not produce the kind of results that a good program requires. The reporting should start at the first line of supervision and pyramid its way to the top. The reports should indicate the overall results and highlight the exceptions. They should reflect the fact that supervision was the first to know when things went wrong, took appropriate action to correct the situation, and minimized problems that occurred. The sketch below reflects the pyramid.

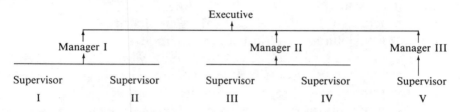

Notice that the arrows all go in an upward direction. Each level of reporting represents the combined bottom line of the level below. Thus, the reports from five supervisors become one report for an executive. The supervisor's report is the cornerstone. Without it, the reports above it cannot be generated.

REVERSE REACTION

In designing the reports in this fashion, each level of management is provided with his or her "needs to know." The manager sees that which his supervisors report, the executive what his managers report. The manager concerns himself with the bottom line of each supervisor's activities and results, the executive with that of the manager. It is expected and anticipated that the role of the executive is to react to the report produced as a composite of his department managers' reports. His reaction or follow-up is a key to the success of the program. Without his follow-up, the program will soon lose momentum and gradually dissipate. Through his follow-up, the program must endure. It cannot break *up*. It can only break *down*. That is the principle of pyramid reporting.

SETTING THE GOALS

The reporting system is designed to reflect accomplishment. The accomplishment can be measured against a goal in terms of actual accomplishments. The goal, in most instances, is the result expected when a given R/E is multiplied by the actual volume. This is often referred to as the plan. The actual volume, of course, is the true result for the reporting period. The difference between the two is the variance and can be expressed as a plus or minus.

An excellent example of this type of reporting, and one that not only reflects the goals but also serves as a good example of the report pyramiding structure, is found in a southeastern hotel chain. After some in-depth studies were done of the time that it takes to clean a room, do the laundry, and inspect the room after it has been made up, a figure of 28 minutes per cleaned room was established. This became the goal. It became incumbent upon each general manager to achieve the goal and report his results.

On a daily basis, at the outset of the program, each of the 70-odd hotels reported their results to the districts, of which there were 8. The districts, in turn, reported their results to the office of the vice president in charge of the program. His office compiled the results into a report that was presented to the executive committee once a week. Many of the hotels quickly achieved the goal without any diminution of company quality requirements. At the outset, many units were not accomplishing results. This was evident in the daily reports to the division managers and was ultimately reflected in the weekly report to the executive committee.

When the vice president reported the chain total, he had to be prepared to pinpoint those districts in which shortfalls occurred and what action was being taken. For this to be done, the district managers had to explain to him what actions were being taken to bring recalcitrant units into line.

There were other aspects to the reporting system concerned with measuring the actual results against the goal. The key to the system's success, in addition to its goals, was that information regarding the individual manager's progress toward meeting the goals was not second hand. He was the first to know because he had to calculate the actual progress and compare it to the goal each day.

TYPES OF GOALS

Goals can be established in terms of labor hours per unit of production, a percentage of achievement, either in terms of utilization of resources, productivity, or both. They can be expressed in terms of dollars, though management usually gets more financial reports than they have time to digest. In most instances, it is best to report in other than financial terms. Achievement will produce the results that will show up on the bottom line of the financial report.

A major oil company, concerned with its extremely heavy expenses in transporting men and materials to and from offshore locations, embarked on a program for reducing its costs. The program called for weekly reporting to management that would reflect how well the program was affecting *boat utilization.*

In the order central department of a large wood products company, *individual productivity* goals were established, and each supervisor's report had to reflect his group's achievement.

A manufacturing company established goals in terms of units produced per man/machine hour and continuously monitored actual production against them.

THE VALUE OF EXAMINING THE PRESENT REPORTING SYSTEMS

Prior to establishing the type of reporting that will reflect the results of the program, it is best to have a complete understanding of the reporting mechanisms already in place. The question should be raised as to their applicability as they exist, or whether they can be changed to achieve the desired results.

One manufacturing company produced a monthly report showing individual productivity. The foreman receiving the report (in the days after the month's end) was supposed to improve the low producers' performance. After the program was installed, he received a daily performance report. Now he was in a position to work closely with his people and to correct conditions more readily. Departmental performance throughout the company improved.

The idea is to avoid having first-line supervisors recapping performance. We want him or her to have early recognition of conditions that adversely affect his or her unit's performance but not spend an inordinate amount of time doing paperwork.

REPORTING AGAINST SPECIFIC GOALS

In many operations, particularly in white-collar activities, the proper economic staffing level (ESL) can be established and the reporting system geared to reflect the department's condition as related to that staffing level. This is particularly true of departments or areas where the volume of work is relatively stable.

For example, in the pathology department of a large New England teaching hospital, the results of the application of a key volume indicator demonstrated that the technicians' economic staffing level was 12 people or 450 hours per week. So the first item on the report compared the actual hours paid to the staffing level

ESL		Hours Distribution			
No.	Hours	Worked	Vacation	Absent	Total
12	450	397.5	37.5	15.0	450

Any deviation immediately alerts management to a problem.

The next step was to demonstrate how well the hours worked were utilized. The hours spent on scheduled work were measured against the total hours worked. The goal was to utilize 85% of the hours on planned or scheduled activities. Thus we have another calculation.

Hours worked	397.5
Hours on scheduled work	342.0
% on scheduled work	86%

This example shows that the goal was achieved and that supervision was actually able to control 86% of the time of the people by giving them assignments with specific time requirements (R/Es).

The next step in the reporting system reflects how well the group performed against the work assignments. The sum total of tests performed is summerized in terms of the R/E. In this case we find that the total was 246 hours. So we have:

Hours on scheduled work	342
Hours of work produced	246
% Performance	72%

The performance goal was established at 90%, so it is evident that actual performance fell far short of the goal.

Assuming that supervisors have been doing their job, they will know the individual work assignment(s) that caused the problem(s) and will have instituted action of a corrective nature as they occurred. Questions that should arise in the mind of the manager of the department are:

1. Were there specific jobs that pulled down the performance?
2. Is there a problem on the part of some individuals?
3. Is it possible that there was not enough work and assignments were stretched out (Parkinson's Law)?
4. Did equipment failure play a part?

The answer to any or all of these questions should be known to the supervisor involved the moment they occurred. Corrective action, to the degree attainable within the supervisor's responsibility and authority should have been taken. Was such action taken? The reporting opens the door for a dialogue between the manager and the supervisor. It gives the manager the opportunity to evaluate the supervisor's awareness and reaction. It also opens the door for constructive advice and for training.

REPORTING AGAINST A VARIABLE VOLUME

As described in previous chapters, the development of an R/E or standard for units of production enables the supervisor to immediately recognize off-schedule conditions on a short-time basis and take corrective action. The calculation is:

$$\text{Actual time} - (\text{R/E} \times \text{volume}) = \pm \text{ difference}$$

In reporting the departmental results, however, the figures are somewhat different because a different expression of the result is desired.

$$(\text{R/E} \times \text{volume}) \div \text{Actual time} = \% \text{ performance}$$

In this manner, the standard time (R/E × volume) can be calculated for varying volume levels and can be divided by the actual time it took to produce that volume. The R/E × volume, in effect, is the standard.

Exhibit 12.1 demonstrates how this standard reflects a performance against a goal that varies with the volume. The exhibit is from the hotel chain mentioned in the section above on "Setting the Goals." Each hotel in the chain reported the data daily from three

COST CENTER	STD HRS	ACT HRS	+/- DIFF	%
HOUSEKEEPING				
RESTAURANT				
GIFT SHOP				
TOTAL				

STANDARD HOURS CALCULATION

HOUSEKEEPING   ROOMS OCCUPIED x 28 ÷ 60

RESTAURANT   GUESTS SERVED AT PEAK x 3 ÷ 60 x MEAL PERIOD HOURS

GIFT SHOP   DOLLAR REVENUE x .011 HOURS

Exhibit 12-1.

key operations. The volumes of these three key cost centers varied daily.

In housekeeping, for example, if the hotel had 90 occupants for the night, the standard labor hours would be 90 × 28 divided by 60 = 42 hours for cleaning rooms, doing the laundry, and inspecting the cleaned rooms. This meant a need for 6 people, each of whom worked a seven hour day. The manager's job was to put in the actual hours, calculate the difference and the percentage of performance against the standard. In this case, both the plus or minus difference and the percentage of performance to standard were used.

BACKLOG DATA IN MANAGEMENT REPORTING

Many operations must be concerned with the amount of work in backlog. Most manufacturing companies keep careful account of the orders in their backlog. Many departments within a company want to see backlog in their staging areas. A given amount of backlog is healthy, and too little can cause interruptions in the work flow, with a resulting loss of man- and machine-time. Too much backlog can mean delays in delivery promises or can extend delivery schedules beyond the point of customer acceptance and result in lost business.

It is important therefore, in many operations, that the backlog be reported as part of the management reporting system. Maintenance operations present a good example of this need, as do many clerical operations. Backlog information must be translated into the hours required to handle the backlog so that decisions can be made to ensure that the facility is adequately equipped.

For example: In a department consisting of 10 people with 375 hours available per week, a backlog of 3750 hours would represent 10 weeks of work. Is this an acceptable backlog? This is a question that can only be answered by management, which therefore has a need to know.

Conversely, if a department loses time waiting for work, then a backlog should exist to run the department in an economic fashion.

CALCULATING THE BACKLOG

At face value, calculating the backlog appears to be a relatively simple process. The R/E per unit multiplied by the number of units in the backlog will give the hours in the backlog. This figure compared to the man- and/or machine-hours available to produce it will demonstrate whether or not the department is in a healthy position. But this is too simple. Additional information is needed.

The percentage of performance of the unit against the standard is required to properly evaluate the backlog. Here's how it works:

Step 1. There are 1000 units of work in the backlog. The R/E is 0.4 hours per unit. This means that there is a standard measure of 400 backlog hours.

Step 2. The departmental performance is running at 85% on a historical basis. Therefore, the 400 backlog hours must be divided by 85% to determine the actual labor hours required. Thus $400 \div 85\% = 470.5$ hours. This is the true value of the backlog.

Step 3. There are eight people in the department available 37.5 hours each, for a total of 300 hours. By dividing the 470.5 by 300, we find that the department has an actual backlog of 1.57 weeks of work.

Exhibit 12.2 is the entire bottom line of the reporting for a given department. The same format could be used to show individual departments with the total representing a larger entity. This format allows for the pyramiding of the reports.

WEEKLY DEPARTMENTAL
MANAGEMENT REPORT

DEPARTMENT:

WEEK ENDING DATE:

SECTION	PERSONNEL/HOURS AVAILABLE					PERFORMANCE				BACKLOG			
	E.S.L.	HOURS WORKED			+/− DIFF	HOURS ON SCHED	SCHED HOURS PRODUCD	% PERF	NON SCHED HOURS	UNITS	HOURS	REQ HOURS	WEEKS
		REG	O.T.	TOTAL									
TOTAL	14	502.5	7.5	510	−15	465	390	83.8%	45 / 9%	3500	1400	1821	3.5

Exhibit 12-2.

total representing a larger entity. This format allows for the pyramiding of the reports.

The *economic staffing level* (ESL) is shown in numbers of people and regular hours. This figure is the budgeted figure for the department. If the budget has been based on a variable volume, that is, hours per unit, the figure may well be a variable. If the budget has been developed on an average basis and is not readily subject to change, then this will be a fixed figure. In the example shown, the figure of 14 people at 37.5 hours per week is a fixed staffing figure.

The actual hours worked are shown in regular and overtime categories to alert management to any serious or continuing overtime situations. In this case, a three day absentee caused 22.5 lost hours. Because 7.5 hours of overtime were used, the total actual hours of 510 resulted in a net loss from the staffing level of 15 hours. This would not be considered serious since it is a loss of less than 3% compared to a plus or minus 5% goal.

The hours on schedule represent the *actual* hours spent on scheduled (measured) work. The *scheduled hours produced* are the result of the volume produced times the R/E. Percentage performance is determined by dividing the scheduled hours produced by the *actual hours on schedule*. The *non-scheduled hours* is the difference between the actual hours on schedule and the total hours worked and is shown in hours and as a percentage.

In the example used, the goal for performance is 90% so the department is below par. The goal for nonscheduled hours is 5% so we have a double below-par situation.

The backlog is shown in units and hours. In the total column or in any area where the backlog is made up of a variety of different units, the unit column is not used. The 3500 units represent 1400 hours of work at an R/E of 0.4 hours per unit.

The required hours needed to complete 1400 hours of work, based on a performance factor of 83.8% is 1671 hours. Since one given week's performance may not be indicative of the general performance of the department, it is recommended that a five week rolling average be used for this calculation.

Another factor has been introduced here—the percentage of nonscheduled hours. Again, a five week rolling average is recommended, although in the example, the current figure is used. To calculate the hours required, an additional 9% is added, which makes the hours required 1821.

Dividing 1821 by the economic staffing level hours, 525, yields 3.5 weeks of work in the department.

MANAGEMENT FOLLOW-UP

The information presented in the report should raise questions on the part of the recipient.

- What caused the low performance and what is being done to improve?
- Why was the goal of 5% nonscheduled hours missed?
- Is three and a half weeks of backlog a healthy situation or not?

Consider the economic impact on the department's operation. If goals had been met, the hours required would come to 1633 (1400 ÷ .9 + .05). The difference of 188 at a cost of approximately $12.00 an hour is $2256 excess. On a continuing basis, this can be a very serious trend.

MANAGEMENT FOLLOW-UP

In the follow-up process, two approaches in particular are essential. First, one must ask, What were the causes of problems, and second, How did supervision handle the developing situations to prevent them from becoming worse and to avoid repetition? This places the first-line supervisor in a position where his supervisory ability and experience are put to the test. If he has followed the program, he will have accounted for the lost performance by job as it occurred. He will have accounted for the time spent on unscheduled work as it occurred. It is management's responsibility to review his records of the events. Again, the questions:

- What happened, by occurrence?
- What did the supervisor do?

In this manner, his effectiveness can be evaluated and improved.

The follow-up process will very quickly reveal the attitude of management collectively or individually. Management styles vary considerably but, as previously mentioned at the beginning of this chapter, will generally reflect the attitude at the top. It is important to recognize that supervision is a part of management. It is *most* important that supervisors recognize that fact and handle themselves as a part of the management team.

ADDITIONAL REPORT SAMPLES

One midwestern manufacturer of animal feeds had, historically, measured its output in tonnage produced. However, it had never thought in terms of labor-hours per ton. In each plant, labor was spread among several departments and functions, both direct and indirect. When the cost improvement program was introduced, each department in each plant was brought into it.

Exhibit 12.3 represents 10 weeks of a weekly report by a plant to the division. The first section shows the weekly tonnage, hours worked, and the man-hours used per ton produced. This is followed by a section showing the base hours per ton (the hours used per ton prior to the program at various production levels). The plus or minus difference is that between the current week's man-hours per ton and the base. This difference is accumulated as the weeks progress.

What the report shows is that the cost (in labor-hours) per ton has decreased as the result of the program. The remaining three sections convert the savings into dollars at the average labor rate of the plant.

Exhibit 12.3 is a good example of how information already available was incorporated into the reporting aspects of the program to tie in with the company's basic philosophy of operation.

In the case of a western life insurance company, top management made a decision that the firm would not reduce employment except by attrition. Their reporting was to reflect the position of each department measured against the economic staffing level and was also to reflect the transfer of hours, performance, and backlog or carry over of the department's key volume item.

In Exhibit 12.4, the *number* of people both exempt (E) and nonexempt (NE) actually employed in the department are listed against the economic staffing level; underwriting, for example, shows two exempt and seven nonexempt positions compared to the economic staffing level of two and five.

The hours of the two E and seven NE staff members are shown including hours absent and transfer hours. The actual hours worked, 292, is figured by adding regular and overtime hours, deducting hours absent, and adding hours transferred in. The distribution of these 292 hours shows 73 fixed (two people) and 210.4 hours spent on

LABOR PERFORMANCE SUMMARY

AVERAGE WAGE = $5.45/HOUR

W/E DATE	TONS PRODUCED	HOURS WORKED	MAN HRS PER TON	BASE PER TON	+/- DIFF	CUM DIFF	CURR. WE. SAVINGS		CUM. SAVINGS		ANNUALIZED SAVINGS	
							HOURS	DOLLARS	HOURS	DOLLARS	HOURS	DOLLARS
3/25	2882	3488	1.35	1.60	−.25	−.25	645.5	3518	645.5	3518	39239	213852
4/1	2540	3632	1.43	1.60	−.17	−.21	431.8	2353	1077.3	5871	32961	179637
4/8	2345	3772	1.61	1.86	−.25	−.22	586.2	3195	1663.5	9066	34531	188194
4/15	1981	2973	1.50	1.65	−.15	−.21	297.2	1620	1960.7	10686	32961	179637
4/22	2329	3477	1.49	1.86	−.37	−.24	559.0	3047	2519.7	13733	37670	205302
4/29	2183	3184	1.46	1.84	−.38	−.26	829.5	4521	3349.2	18254	40809	222409
5/6	2203	3138	1.42	2.0	−.58	−.30	1277.7	6963	4626.9	25217	47087	256625
5/13	2164	3281	1.50	1.84	−.34	−.31	735.7	4009	5362.6	29226	48657	265181
5/20	2174	2776	1.28	1.84	−.56	−.34	1217.4	6635	6580	35861	53365	290839
5/27	2318	3378	1.46	1.84	−.38	−.34	878.2	4786	7458.2	40647	53365	290839

Exhibit 12-3.

Department	STAFF				PAYROLL HOURS					AVAIL. HOURS DISTRIBTUION			PERFORMANCE		CARRY/OVER HOURS	
	ACT		ESL		REG.	O.T.	ABS.	TRANSFER	TOTAL	FIXED	NON-SCHED.	VAR.	E/H	ATTAIN:	Beg.	END
	E	NE	E	NE												
Underwriting	2	7	2	5.0	328.5	18.5	19.0	24.0	292.0	73.0	8.6	210.4	207.6	99%	29.2	30.5
Policyholder Service	1.0	8.0	1.0	7.0	328.6	—	5.6	(2.5)	320.4	36.5	12.0	271.9	258.2	95%	46.0	47.2
Premium Accounting	2	10	2	8.0	365.0	.8	8.0	32.3	390.1	73.0	13.7	303.4	215.3	71%	26.6	36.3
Internal Accounting																
Group	2	4.6	2	4.0	219.0	4.5	—	—	223.5	73.0	6.0	144.5	125.5	87%	7.7	14.5
EDP	1	8	.3	8.0	328.5	—	—	—	328.5	182.5	6.0	140.0	165.2	118%	—	—
Programming																
Claims	2	6	2.0	6	292.0	1.4	20.8	—	272.6	73.0	27.8	171.8	178.8	104%	6.8	7.1
Office Services																
Building Services																
Mort. Loan Investments																
Actuarial																
Agency																
TOTAL	10	43	9.3	38	1,861.5	25.2	113.4	53.8	1,827.1	511.0	74.1	1,242.0	1,150.6	93%		

Exhibit 12–4.

DEPARTMENTAL OPERATING REPORT

DEPARTMENT: _UNDERWRITING_   WEEK ENDING:

DAY	STAFF		PAYROLL HOURS					AVAIL. HOURS DISTRIBUTION			PERFORMANCE		C/O HOURS	
	EXEMPT	NON-EXEMPT	REG.	O.T.	ABS.	TRANSFER	TOTAL	FIXED	NON-SCHED.	VAR.	E/H	ATTAIN:	BEG	END
MONDAY	2	7	72.0	5.1	(8.0)		69.1	16.0	1.8	51.3	41.3	81	29.2	
TUESDAY	2	7	72.0	3.3	(15.0)		60.3	16.0	1.5	42.8	43.2	101		
WEDNESDAY	2	7	72.0	2.0	(24.0)	13.0	63.0	16.0	2.0	45.0	40.3	90		
THRUSDAY	2	7	72.0	3.3	(24.0)	11.0	62.3	16.0	1.2	45.1	44.4	98		
FRIDAY	2	7	40.6	4.8	(8.0)		37.3	9.0	2.1	26.2	38.4	147		30.5
SATURDAY														
TOTALS	2	7	328.5	18.5	(79.0)	24.0	292.0	73.0	8.6	210.4	207.6	99		

COMMENTS: FRIDAY 2/7 – HI ATTAINMENT CAUSED BY INCONSISTENT STANDARD. NEEDS REVISING.

REVIEWED BY: _____

Exhibit 12-5.

scheduled work. Only 8.6 hours were not scheduled. The 210.4 hours produced 207.6 hours of work for an attainment of 99%. The report also shows that the week began with 29.2 hours of backlog and ended with 30.5, a minor change. The bottom line of the report (which shows that not all of the departments were on the program at that point in time) indicates a current overstaffing of 0.7 exempt and 5 nonexempt personnel.

By way of review, the corresponding report from the underwriting department has been included (Exhibit 12.5) to illustrate that the supervisor maintains his control and performance on a daily basis and the report pyramids in an upward direction. The note on the report for Friday demonstrates the supervisor's concern that the report reflects a need for some possible revision of standard data (R/Es) in his department.

Feeding information into a management report directly from individual performances is illustrated in Exhibit 12.6. This particular example comes from a telephone company network operation in which a field engineering foreman lays out his plan for each of his

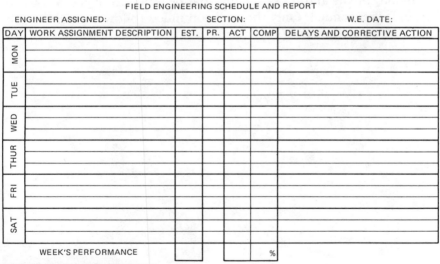

FIELD ENGINEERING SCHEDULE AND REPORT

ENGINEER ASSIGNED: SECTION: W.E. DATE:

DAY	WORK ASSIGNMENT DESCRIPTION	EST.	PR.	ACT	COMP	DELAYS AND CORRECTIVE ACTION
MON						
TUE						
WED						
THUR						
FRI						
SAT						

WEEK'S PERFORMANCE   %

BEGINNING B/L HOURS	
+ INPUT HOURS	
− COMPLETED HOURS	
ENDING BACKLOG HRS.	

Exhibit 12–6.

field men for the week. Each assignment is listed, estimated, and given its priority. The engineer fills in the actual hours spent on each assignment and checks off the job when completed. His activities are reviewed daily and appropriate adjustments made.

At week's end, the estimated hours and actual hours spent on *completed* jobs are summarized and the performance percentage calculated. The backlog data are filled in and the report submitted to the coordinator who summarizes the sections in a station report. The station reports are summarized in a district report. The bottom line of each district report becomes a report for the vice president of engineering.

SUMMARY

When the program is integrated into the full company operation, consideration must be given to what management believes is its "needs to know" to evaluate results and track progress. Management will react to the reporting function according to its own philosophy of operation. A successful program depends on the attention of management and its belief that the benefits produced are worth the effort expended. Only through continued follow-up will the program be perpetuated.

13

A Case History

This chapter is actually from an instruction manual of a program for improved labor utilization developed for a major oil company at its offshore facilities in the Gulf of Mexico. This particular situation was chosen because it represents not only the basic principles of improving the productive output of a labor group but also involves some unique aspects of control and follow-up.

An analysis revealed an operation covering more than twenty thousand miles of open water with production facilities stretching from the Texas coast to the gulf area south of eastern Louisiana. It involved seven production "units," each containing a number of production "platforms" through which oil and gas flow from the undersea wells. The platforms and the well heads require continuing operational procedures and maintenance.

The company was concerned that the facilities were not being maintained as well as they might and that the labor crews were not fully employed. The analysis brought home the point by revealing a lost time ratio of more than 50%, a good portion of which could be credited to the failure to plan the activities of personnel on a day-to-day basis. This was of particular concern since the people actually lived at the offshore facilities for seven straight days. Crew changes occurred every seven days with a complete change of foremen as well as workers. Continuity of work between crews needed improvement.

The analysis also revealed that the idle or lost time among the people was a detriment to morale. Boredom can be a real problem.

In the pages that follow, the complete system that was developed is shown. This chapter is different than most in that it is a complete instructional manual of the procedures implemented. The ultimate result was, and is, a vastly improved operational and maintenance program that helped reduce well down-time and assisted in slowing the deterioration of these offshore facilities in the midst of a highly corrosive environment.

SYSTEM SYNOPSIS

The Offshore Operations and Maintenance Control System was designed for the *operations foreman* to assist him in accomplishing his assigned responsibilities. The operations foreman is the cornerstone on which planned production, effective maintenance, and adherence to regulations depends. In addition, he is responsible for the effectiveness of his assigned personnel, for their morale and training, and for their accomplishment of work in a safe and mature manner. The goal of the system is to provide the operations foreman with the tools he needs to meet these responsibilities.

The procedures that follow explain *how* to use the tools; this synopsis explains *why* the system was designed and *what* control the operations foreman can obtain through his conscientious use of the system. The system has three basic elements:

1. Weekly platform inspections by the operations foreman
2. A complete *Work List* of work to be done on the platforms
3. A *Daily Work Report* from the employees on the work performed that day

In order for the operations foreman to assign and control the work accomplished in the field, he must first identify it. By conducting a thorough *inspection* of each of his assigned platforms, at least weekly, he can determine the work required to be done. Additionally, while on the platforms, he can increase his rapport with the assigned personnel, conduct training and safety meetings, and follow up on the quantity and quality of work done since his last inspection. Specific problems can be discussed with the employees in order to enhance the operations foreman's analysis of the Daily Work Reports he has received and to further interpret this information. The operations foreman can therefore grow in his ability to plan work and to set goals for his employees.

The weekly platform inspections enable the operations foreman to construct a detailed, in-depth *Work List* of work requirements by platform. The operations foreman uses the Work List to both plan and schedule the work; with the reading of the appropriate Daily Work Reports, he is able to interpret what he planned versus what was accomplished, and when he scheduled the work to be done versus when the work was done. He also has the ability of prioritizing the work, of directing the sequence in which the work is performed.

Work accomplishments are recorded on the *Daily Work Reports*. These reports explain to the operations foreman what happened on the platform that day; what transpired that helped or hindered the employees' accomplishments. In addition, the reports should answer some other questions for the operations foreman:

- Did the employees accomplish what was planned?
- What other work did they do?
- Did they find and note problems and abnormalities?
- Did they explain why the work required more or less time than planned?
- Did they discover additional work to be done later, either by themselves or by those with special talents?
- What are the "red flags" that the operations foreman can make use of on his other platforms?

The Daily Work Reports should be written in sufficient detail to allow the operations foreman to interpret answers to the above questions.

In order for the operations foreman to grow professionally, he must master the many and varied aspects of his position. The system assists him to plan and schedule better, to inspect more thoroughly and consistently, and to identify and solve operating problems in the field. Basically, the operations foreman increases his control over the work efforts on his platforms. Less is left to chance. By becoming a better planner and scheduler and by following up on work efforts more, he is also making his employees aware of his expectations. This will ultimately increase not only the work efforts themselves, but the quality of the work as well.

SYSTEM RESPONSIBILITIES

A. *Field Personnel.* To provide the operations foreman with a concise and accurate report of their work accomplishments for the day. Work of a "routine" nature need not be reported daily, but problems or abnormalities noted as a result of routine surveillance walk-throughs should be noted.

B. *Operations Foreman.* To use the system to identify, plan, schedule, prioritize, and monitor work accomplishments of his personnel. This is done by:

1. Conducting detailed inspections of each of the assigned platforms at least weekly; noting and assigning work to be accomplished
2. Reviewing work reports to note accomplishments, monitoring hours required for the completion of jobs, and identifying potential problem areas
3. Evaluating preventive maintenance card completions weekly.
4. Verifying verbally that daily routine activities are being conducted with the thoroughness demanded by the operations foreman

C. *Production Foreman.* The system was designed to assist the operations foreman accomplish his responsibilities (see Ex. 13.1). The production foreman, however, is directly responsible for the effectiveness, quality, and perpetuation of the system. He is also instrumental in guiding the operations foremen, from a *unit* viewpoint, in establishing consistency in planning, scheduling, and monitoring techniques, and in the effectiveness of the reporting. On a weekly basis, the production foreman reviews in detail the Work Lists and the Daily Work Reports of each of his operations foremen. During the weekly reviews, the production foreman should note:

1. Work planned (Work List) versus work accomplished (Daily Work Reports), and the reasons therefor.
2. Estimated hours versus actual hours required. Is there another problem here?
3. Quality and quantity of unscheduled work reported.

Offshore Operations and Maintenance Control System–System Flow

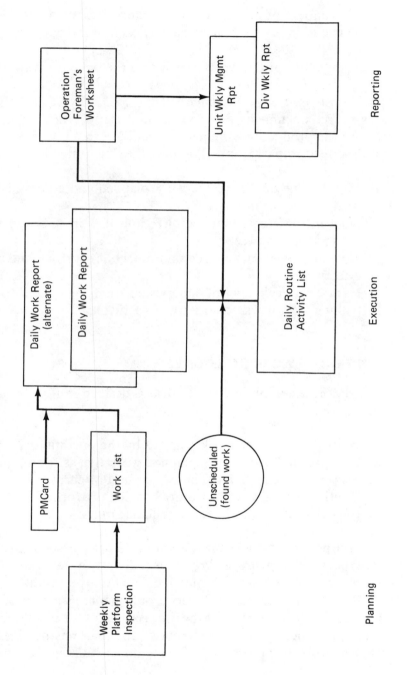

Exhibit 13-1.

4. The amount of preventive maintenance done on a weekly basis.
5. The amount of backlog carried by each of the operations foremen.
6. The quality of the work planned by the operations foremen.

D. *Production Superintendent.* To periodically review the system's source documents (Work Lists and Daily Work Reports) on site with the production foreman. In addition to a review similar to that described in paragraph C, above, the Superintendent should:

1. Monitor the quality of the work planned and accomplished in light of long-term goals
2. Note inconsistencies in the direction of work planned within the unit and between units
3. Note improvements in accomplishments, reporting, and system effectiveness
4. Ensure, at each level of supervision, that the system for controlling field work activities is perpetuated

DEFINITION OF WORK CATEGORIES

Work that is accomplished in the field is defined in four broad categories:

1. *Work list items,* or work planned by the operations foreman
2. *Unscheduled work,* or unplanned work that is found on site
3. *Preventive maintenance,* noted on the PM cards
4. Routine, or daily work required by the platforms, such as the lease operator's platform surveillance tours

The purpose of categorizing the work is to determine, by platform, where the work emphasis is. When the majority of the available time is spent on work list items, it may indicate that the operations foreman is conducting good inspections and planning his work properly. When a major portion of the time is categorized as unscheduled, it tends to indicate that the operations foreman has not identified sufficient work to productively fill the time available. Limited pre-

ventive maintenance entries could mean that the employees are let-
ting the PM slip, which would necessitate a period of "catch-up"
time toward the end of the month. A high percentage of routine
effort indicates that a large portion of the day's work effort is neither
controlled nor directed by the operations foreman.

More detailed definitions of the work categories follow:

A. *Work list items.* That work identified and planned by the operations foreman in advance of assigning the work to his personnel,
excluding routine and preventive maintenance work. Each work list
item has a number assigned by the operations foreman to identify
that work by platform. Further, he estimates the time that will be
required to accomplish the work and, following its completion, compares the total actual hours that are required to accomplish the work
to his estimate.

B. *Unscheduled work.* That work accomplished by the employee
while on the job of which the operations foreman had no prior
knowledge. This work is not estimated, but is entered on the Daily
Work Report with a brief description and the actual hours that were
required. Note that when work is found and accomplished by the
employee as a result of a routine surveillance tour or a preventive
maintenance assignment, that work and the hours expended are entered on the Daily Work Report as unscheduled work (no item number).

C. *Preventive maintenance cards.* That work performed in ac-
cordance with the PM card instructions. The preventive maintenance
cards are issued to the platforms weekly by the operations foreman.
PM standard hours, hours deemed appropriate for the accomplishment of the PM activity and assigned by the Maintenance Support
Group, are noted on the cards. Employees note that preventive maintenance activities are completed and record the actual hours used on
the Daily Work Report.

D. *Routine.* Routine work includes repetitive activities that are required to be done daily on the platforms. Routine work, for the purpose of the system, is as follows:

- The lease operator's platform surveillance tours
- Daily production reporting activities
- Cooking meals and doing laundry, on selected platforms

WEEKLY PLATFORM INSPECTION GUIDELINE

PURPOSE   To provide a guideline for the operations foreman's weekly platform inspection. Further it provides consistency of inspecting by hitch and by unit throughout the Gulf.

RESPONSIBILITY   The operations foreman is responsible for conducting weekly inspections on all of his assigned platforms.

FREQUENCY   Each platform is inspected once per hitch.

DISTRIBUTION   The Weekly Platform Inspection Guidelines for each assigned platform reviewed with the production foreman weekly, together with the review of the Work Lists and the Daily Work Reports. The guidelines are then filed for one year with the production foreman to be used as backup, if required, in supplying information to MMS, USCG, and so on.

PREPARATION   Refer to the blank guideline (Exhibit 13.2), keyed to the following:

1. *HEADING.* Pertinent information regarding the platform description, the date of the inspection, and the name of the Operations Foreman conducting the inspection.
2. *YES/NO.* Enter as appropriate. Abnormalities should be explained in the Remarks section, as well as added to the Operations Foreman's Work List to assure that the work is planned and completed.
3. *REMARKS.* On a separate sheet, note items in need of correction, such as, unsafe conditions, unsafe operations, inadequacies, etc.

Note: Should there be additional items to be inspected, unique to a platform, the items should be discussed with the production foreman and, if appropriate, added to the guideline.

WORK LIST

PURPOSE   To provide a working document for the operations foreman to ensure that all ongoing work required on each platform and jacket for which he is responsible is controlled. The Work List is updated regularly as a result of the operations foreman's in-depth weekly platform inspections and, therefore, is prepared and maintained for each platform or work location. Additionally, the Work List provides the production foreman with a view of the quantity and quality of work that is planned and performed on the platforms, as well as providing the men responsible for the platform/jacket with a view of the work that is planned. The work entered on the Work List is *all* work that the platform requires. Work exceeding the abilities of the operations foreman's assigned complement, such as wireline, MSG-type work or capital work, should be discussed with the production foreman.

PLATFORM: ① _____
DATE: _____
OPS FM: _____

		YES	NO
1.	**SAFETY AND ENVIRONMENTAL.**		
	a. Life rafts, rings, jackets: Clean, properly identified and stored, in adequate supply and condition. OIL 4.14.	②	
	b. Hearing protection: Provided in high noise areas; used.		
	c. Eye Protection: Provided near grinders, buffers; used.		
	d. Navigational aide: All operational.		
	e. Fire and work permits: Issued, OIL 4.03.		
	f. Flanges: Open flanges on platform.		
	g. Vibrations: Any obvious, serious vibrations. SEC 1.01.1a.		
	h. Gas detectors: Operational.		
	i. Halon system: Operational.		
	j. Daily Operating Reports: Review all daily operating reports for major pieces of equipment for completeness, abnormalities and trends.		
	k. Safety devices: In service. When temporarily by-passed, is operator or designate in constant attendance. Are "Out of Service" signs being used. Oil 8.02.		
	l. Safety meetings: Held weekly. Operations Foreman present. Minutes sent in.		
	m. Capsule or watercraft drills: Conducted by each crew. Report sent in.		
	n. Required safety signs: Installed. SEC 2.01.7 and 2.01.8.		
2.	**PRODUCTION AND SURVEILLANCE.**		
	a. Tubing and casing pressures: Checked as required.		
	b. Production Reports: Correct and complete.		
	c. Well tests: (OIL 1.26 and 1.27)		
	(1) Wells tested on a regular basis.		
	(2) Test reports correct and complete. Signed by Lease Operator.		
	d. Flare indicators: In continuous service. Flare point shown on chart daily.		
	e. Gas measurement:		
	(1) Meters zeroed daily.		
	(2) Orifice plate sized correctly; differential in 40" to 80" range.		
	f. Swab valves: Closed, except when checking tubing pressure or working on well.		
3.	**EQUIPMENT.**		
	a. Grating: Secured properly; free of holes; barricades used when grating is temporarily removed.		
	b. WEMCO: Hatches secured tightly,		
	c. Handrails: No void spaces; socketed adequately.		
	d. Bleed valves: Piped directly to skid pans; plugged, if not in regular use. SEC 1.02.5g.		
	e. Drains: Operational. SEC 1.02.5k.		
	f. Flange bolts: Missing; tight.		
	g. Sight glasses; Clean.		
	h. Gauge columns: Easily operated.		
	i. Diesel engines: Exhausts equipped with spark arrestors; batteries enclosed.		
4.	**NAVIGATIONAL AIDS.** (OIL 5.03 and SEC 1.18.10g)		
	a. Fog horn: Operational.		
	b. Navigational lights: Operational.		
	c. Identification signs: Present.		
	d. Reflective tape on flare piles: Present.		
5.	**CRANE OPERATIONS.**		
	a. Personnel net: In good condition; used strictly for personnel; OIL 4.06.		
	b. Crane boom: In cradle when crane is idle.		
	c. Cables in good condition.		
	d. Operating instructions: Posted in crane.		
	e. Operator: Crane operated only by qualified personnel, qualified operators noted on Qualification Record.		
	f. Inspection: Crane inspection up to date.		
6.	**WIRELINE OPERATIONS.**		
	a. Lubricator: Tested per OIL 3.82.		
	b. Briefing: Lease Operators and Wireline Operators briefed relative to the job at hand, well conditions, etc.		
	c. Coverage: The well is attended full time throughout wireline operation by wireline crew.		
	d. A–Frame: Properly secured by wireline crew.		
	e. Christmas Tree: Properly cleaned by wireline crew at the completion of the job.		

Exhibit 13–2.

Note: An in-depth sample Work List is shown in Exhibits 13.3a and b. The sample Work List tracks with the sample Daily Work Report (see Exs. 13.4a & b).

RESPONSIBILITY The operations foreman is responsible for entering all on-going work to be accomplished on the Work List. The sources for identifying work to be done and added to the Work List are varied:

1. The operations foreman, as a result of his weekly inspections in the field
2. The production foreman, as a result of his field visits
3. The personnel assigned to the platform, as a result of routine walk-throughs and his or her on-going watching and listening done as an integral part of the position

FREQUENCY The Work List should be updated each hitch, by the incoming operations foreman.

DISTRIBUTION The original is maintained by the operations foreman. A copy is available at the work location. An additional copy is forwarded to the production foreman. Any updating (additions or completion dates) to the Work List is done by the operations foreman, who transfers the updating information to the production foreman, and the affected platform.

PREPARATION Refer to the blank control (Exs. 13a & b), keyed to the following:

1. *PLATFORM(S)*. As a separate Work List is prepared for each platform, or work location, enter the name of the platform, or the names of the platforms, in the complex.
2. *ITEM NO.* All work to be accomplished is assigned in numerical sequence. In order to avoid unwieldy numbers, it is thought that the numbers can be repeated quarterly without confusion.
3. *ASG.* When the operations foreman assigns the work, he notes this fact by entering a checkmark in this column. Additionally, the initials of the individual(s) or the job classification assigned the task may be entered here.
4. *DATE ENTER.* The operations foreman adds the date the work is entered on the Work List.
5. *DATE COMPLETED.* The date the work is actually completed is entered in this column. (source: Daily Work Report).
6. *EST HOURS.* The operations foreman records his estimate of the man-hours required to perform the planned work.
7. *ACT HOURS.* The operations foreman enters the actual hours it took to complete the planned work. (source: Daily Work Report).
8. *DESCRIPTION OF WORK.* The operations foreman records the details of the work planned.
9. *REMARKS.* The Operations Foreman planning the work enters any specific tools, talent, safety factors, etc., required to complete the assignment. He may use this column to assign specific individuals or groups of individuals to perform the work. Further, he may add specifics noted on the Daily Work Reports after the job was completed for future reference.

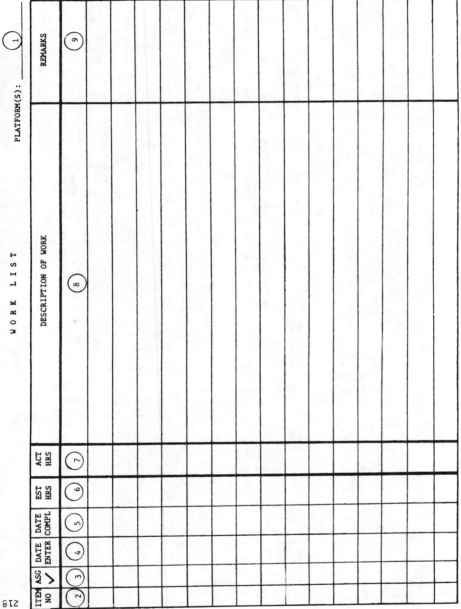

Exhibit 13-3A.

WORK LIST

PLATFORM(S): 58C

ITEM NO	ASG ✓	DATE ENTER	DATE COMPL	EST HRS	ACT HRS	DESCRIPTION OF WORK	REMARKS
1	LO MM	9/1	9/3	2	2	Remove Fisher 2100 level controller s/down on CPI. Not required here.	
2	LO	9/1	9/3	3	2	Replace tubing connections and valves on condensate sales pumps, per M.S.G. Bulletin #31.	
3	LO MM	9/1	9/3	1	2	Replace manual valve on 2″ diesel fuel line with recommended check valve, per M.S.G. Bulletin #36.	
4	LO MM	9/1	9/3	2	4	Install E.S.D. shut in lines, to heliport and capsule, for temporary generator. These are remote shut down lines. Also need to identify these stations with temporary signs.	Had to cut hose end and reclamp connection. Hose worn.
5	LO	9/1	9/3	1	1	Lenses on Mercury Vapor lights at SW lower well bay and NW corner of quarters building are cracked and may no longer be explosion-proof, per S.E.C. #1.06.	
6	CSI Cont	9/1	9/3	8	12	Replace cable to platform lights from junction box to light, with CLX cable, per S.E.C. #1.06. (10 lights total)	
7	SPL Cont	9/1	9/3	Day Rate		Have SPL seal both condensate allocation meters at counter head on AGT as per O.C.S. Order #13.	Had SPL catch gas and water sample. Note: 33.3° API Gvty

Exhibit 13-3B.

DAILY WORK REPORT

PURPOSE
To provide the operations foreman with a document that reports all work activities for the day by platform or work location. To serve as an input to the Work List and provide the operations foreman with the means of evaluating his plan against actual accomplishments.

Note: An in-depth sample Daily Work Report appears in Exhibits 13.4a and b. The sample Daily Work Report tracks with the sample Work List (see Exs. 13.3a and b).

RESPONSIBILITY
It is the responsibility of the individual employee (employees) to briefly describe the detail of all work performed during the day, other than those predetermined routine activities.

FREQUENCY
The Daily Work Report is generated on a daily basis.

DISTRIBUTION
The Daily Work Report is to be telecopied daily to the operations foreman, where possible. If telecopying capabilities are unavailable, the operations foreman is informed by telephone and the Daily Work Report is mailed to him through the internal mailing system.

PREPARATION
Refer to the blank control (Exs. 13.4a and b), keyed to the following:

1. *NAME(S)*. Enter the name or names of the employee(s) preparing the report.
2. *DATE*. Enter the current date.
3. *PLAT NO*. Enter the platform on which the work is performed. Personnel who work on several platform/jackets throughout the day should record their time on the Daily Work Report for the major platform or work location, and use the Daily Work Report (Alternate) to give their operations foreman the detail of the work that was accomplished.

Note: The following four paragraphs concern the daily recording of all hours available to the platform for work on this date. For the purpose of this report, 7 and 7 employees are available for 12 hours of work; 5 and 2 employees for 8 hours. Available hours are only listed in the top portion of the first page of the Daily Work Report. Therefore, on subsequent pages, the work performed may commence at the top of the page.

4. List the names of all regularly assigned hourly employees as well as visitors who spent time on the platform this date.
5. *REG HRS*. Enter available regular hours by individual.
6. *O/T HRS*. Enter actual overtime hours used by individual.
7. Total each category of hours (regular and overtime) to determine the total hours available for work on the platform on this date.

Note: Supervisory and management hours should be included in parentheses, not added into the total available hours.

8. *ITEM NO*. Use *only* when accomplishing Work List assignments.

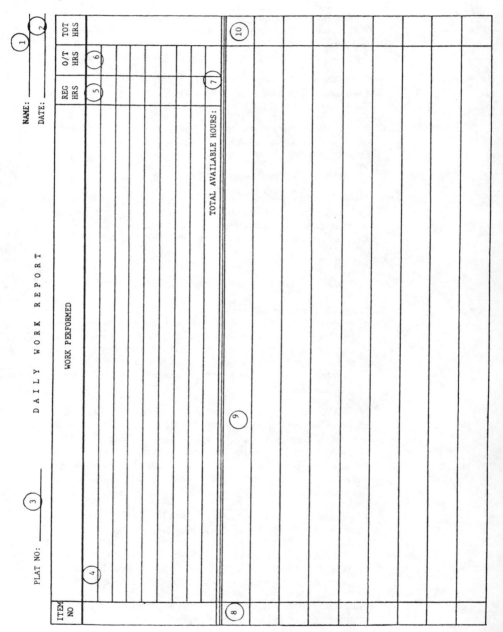

Exhibit 13–4A.

DAILY WORK REPORT

NAME: PETE BROWN
DATE: _____

ITEM NO	WORK PERFORMED	REG HRS	O/T HRS	TOT HRS
	R. Smith – TLO – Overtime to unload Otis and McCullough units.	12	2	
	J. Jones – MMC	12	–	
	S. Moors – MMC – Overtime to unload Otis and McCullough units.	12	2	
	T. Henry – TLO (nights)	12	–	
	H. Thomas – CSI Electrician 12 hrs @ $31/hr = Total: $372.00	12	–	
	B. Frank – SPL Meter 12 hrs minimum @ $420.00	12	–	
	J. White – N. Brown – MMS (3 hrs)			
	R. Black – Company Production Engineer (12 hrs)			
	TOTAL AVAILABLE HOURS	72	4	
1	Removed Fisher 2100 level shut down, low, on CPI and blinded.			2
2	Replaced tubing connections and valves on condensate sales pumps, per MSG Bulletin #31.			2
3	Installed strataflo check valve on diesel fuel hose used to fill tank, per MSG Bulletin #36.			2
	Completed PM Cards on capsule, crane, fire extinguisher. Reports completed (Night man)			2
	Unloaded Otis and McCullough equipment from M/V Timbalier Champion and took on diesel fuel – 400 gal. Night man and two day shift employees.			6
	MMS pre-inspection walk-through. Items noted: A. Crane needs API Certification papers. B. Determine if Transco has waivers on gas detectors in meter building. (complete)			3
	Company in-house training (Jones and Moors)			2

Exhibit 13–4B.

The item number corresponds to the item number on the operations foreman's Work List, and is recorded here.

9. *WORK PERFORMED.* Enter a description of the work performed for the day. It should be as concise as possible, yet sufficient to inform the operations foreman of the status of the assigned work (see Ex. 13.4 for examples). Additionally, when work is accomplished, other than Work List items or routine work, describe the work and leave the item number blank (this would include all unscheduled and preventive maintenance work). Also, note any other work required, or materials required, which should be planned for some future time. This feedback loop provides the operations foreman with information that will assist his future planning. Do not include time waiting for transportation or travel time. These times should be noted in the body of the report, but should *not* be included in the total hours column.

10. *TOT HRS.* Record the total hours worked on the assignment, whether the work was completed or not. The total hours column reflects the total man hours, *not* the total clock hours, worked on the assignment. Example: Three employees worked two hours on an assignment. The total hours column reflects the total of six man hours.

PREVENTIVE MAINTENANCE CARDS

PURPOSE   To provide the operations foreman with his quarterly preventive maintenance requirements on preprinted cards, so that the PM can be planned, accomplished, and reported to the operations foreman on a weekly basis. Additionally, completed preventive maintenance provides both the production foreman and the production superintendent with means to identify preventive maintenance accomplishments on a weekly, monthly, and quarterly basis.

RESPONSIBILITY   The operations foreman is responsible for assigning, monitoring, and reviewing preventive maintenance plans and accomplishments on a weekly basis.

ANALYSIS   The personnel assigned preventive maintenance activities are responsible for completing the PM assignments, as well as recording their preventive maintenance efforts on the Daily Work Reports. The assigned personnel should make notations on the card itself of any information that would make the card more informative as to the true maintenance requirements. The operations foreman approves the revisions and sends the updated cards to MSG under separate cover.

It is imperative that the preventive maintenance be performed during the week in which it is scheduled. At no time should the cards accumulate from hitch to hitch, as it defeats the purpose of establishing planned frequencies to do the work.

DAILY ROUTINE ACTIVITY CHECKLIST

PURPOSE To provide the operations foreman with a guideline of specific items that should be frequently and routinely checked on his platforms. This guideline is to be used by the operations foreman to tailor a checklist for each of his platforms based on major pieces or groups of existing platform equipment. In this manner, good and effective daily routine checks are established on a checklist for each platform within the Division. The checklist serves as an adjunct to daily operating reports, such as generator and crane reports, to ensure the best and most meaningful utilization of the time of assigned personnel (Ex. 13.5).

RESPONSIBILITIES The *operations foreman* builds the checklists for his platforms and forwards copies to the production foreman for his review.

The operations foreman reviews completed checklists, in conjunction with his weekly platform inspection and his review of the daily operating reports. The purpose of his review of vital temperatures, pressures, levels, etc., is to analyze current trends and to assess general operating conditions.

The responsibility of the *lease operators* is to perform the checks daily throughout their hitch. All abnormalities and problems discovered as a result of the routine checks, not otherwise noted on the Daily Work Report, should be entered in a remarks section on the checklist or on a separate sheet.

FREQUENCY Once the checklists are finalized by the operations foreman, the checklists need only be revised with the addition or deletion of equipment.

PREPARATION The operations foreman should build his checklists (1) consistent with the existing platform equipment, and (2) in line with the physical layout of the platform. Note that the frequency of some routine checks may vary with the desires of the production foreman or superintendent. The amount of time required to complete the routine check is established by the operations foreman using the attached guideline for equipment times and the physical layout of the platform for tour times.

The individuals completing the activities listed on the Daily Routine Activity Checklist record their initials as the check is performed in the column under the appropriate day of the hitch.

OPERATIONS FOREMAN'S WORKSHEET

PURPOSE To provide the operations foreman with a timely and concise record of the accomplishments of his assigned platforms for a given day. A separate *Worksheet* is maintained for each platform or work location. In addition, the Worksheets inform the Operations Foreman of how

DAILY ROUTINE ACTIVITY CHECKLIST

		HRS	DAY OF HITCH						
UNIT: _____ Page i of 4 PLATFORM(S):			1	2	3	4	5	6	7
1. Make initial round; inspect and function test safety system.		1							
2. Review and analyze all daily reports.		1							
3. Check all Gas Charts as follows:		1							
a. Assure all charts are inking neatly.									
b. All differentials above 40″.									
c. Zero all meters under pressure.									
d. All meters clean, inside and out.									
e. All sight glasses clean and indicating true level.									
f. All orifice plates stored in wooded boxes.									
4. Check operation of LACT meters/units as follows:		¼							
a. Pans clean, meters clean, no leaks.									
b. Shake-outs taken as required.									
c. B, S&W Monitors in service and working.									
d. Check level in automatic sampler to assure proper operation.									
e. Check pump rate in BBLs/Min to Sales to assure pipeline pumps are pumping through meter at design rate.									
5. Test Wells:		½							
a. Zero both oil and gas meters.									
b. Purge separator adequately before placing well on test.									
c. Install 1/8″ orifice plate in meter run before placing well on test to determine if any valves are leaking on manifold.									
d. Take an adequate number of shake-outs during test to assure shake-out is representative.									
e. Assure all sight glasses are clean.									
f. Check last date of fluid meter calibration. Calibrate, if necessary. (Weekly)		1							
g. Check orifice plate for quality before installing in meter run.									
h. Spare plates picked up and stored in wooden boxes.									
i. All meter and control boxes clean, inside and out.									
j. Test shut down valve to vessel for holding. (Weekly)									
6. Check Production Separators:									
a. All glasses cleaned and zeroed for range.									
b. Gas meters zeroed, clean.									
c. All control boxes clean, inside and out.									
d. Check operation of dump valves. (Weekly)		½							
7. Check operation of Survival Capsule:		½							
a. Check water, oil, fuel, fuel, batteries, radios.									
b. Start and run engine (Check for regulation life jackets).									
c. Lower 8′ to 10′, check cable, winches, rewind.									
d. Check limit switches.									
e. Conduct drill, as per OIL. (Weekly)									
8. Check Platform Drain Systems:		½							
a. Any leaks.									
b. Any system plugged.		¼							
9. Air Packages:									
a. Check and record all operating pressures and temperatures; note any abnormalities on Daily Air Package Report.		¼							
b. Check oil levels.									
c. Bleed water from tanks.									
d. Check level of coolant.									
e. Check all valves for proper operation.									
10. Generators:									
a. Check and record all operating pressures and temperatures; note any abnormalities on Daily Generator Report.		½							
b. Clean floors, walls, cabinets.									
c. Wipe down any oil leaks.									
d. Check all batteries.									

Exhibit 13-5.

the available hours of the day were used and of the proper crewing level for his platforms, his estimated hours to the actual hours required, and update the Work List backlog information.

RESPONSIBILITY It is the responsibility of the employees completing Daily Work Reports to furnish specific information to the operations foreman daily, either telephonically or by telecopier.

The operations foreman is responsible for maintaining his Worksheets, and performing an on-going, in-depth analysis of the status of his platform work and the use being made of the hours available to him for the accomplishment of his duties.

FREQUENCY The operations foreman should keep his Worksheets current daily, summarizing them at the conclusion of his hitch.

DISTRIBUTION At the completion of the hitch, a copy is made of the Worksheets and forwarded through the production foreman to the production superintendent for review. In addition, copies are forwarded to the Maintenance Support Group for inclusion of the information in the division manager's Weekly Management Report.

PREPARATION Refer to the blank control (Exs. 13.6a and b) keyed to the following:

1. *PLATFORM(S)*. List the platform, or work location, applicable to the Worksheet.
2. *UNIT*. The appropriate unit name.
3. *OPNS FOREMAN*. The name of the operations foreman, or acting operations foreman, completing this week's Worksheet.
4. *DATE*. Enter the dates.
   a.–f. Contractor Employees Work Classifications. Listed under subparagraphs a through f, are the types of work classifications used. Note that subparagraph c lists ACR and other Specialists. To be included in this category are instrumentation men, crane mechanics, pump specialists, and so on. In the block provided, by day, enter the hours worked by each contractor for the day.
   g. *SUBTOTAL*. Add entries in subparagraphs a through f, above, and enter total. Note that the totals include overtime hours. (Source: Daily Work Reports).
   h. *EMPLOYEES*. Enter the total hours worked by employees for the day. Note that the total includes overtime hours. (Source: Daily Work Reports).
   i. *TOTAL AVAILABLE HOURS*. Enter the total of the above two entries.
   j. EQUIVALENT PEOPLE. Divide the total available hours by 12 and enter the equivalent people available for work for the day.
5. *TOT HRS*. Summarize the total available hours for the hitch in each category. Note that for equivalent people for the hitch, the total available hours are divided by 84 hours (7 days × 12 hours per day).

The following paragraphs concern the distribution of the hours worked, and other elements important to the operations foreman's analysis of the day's activities.

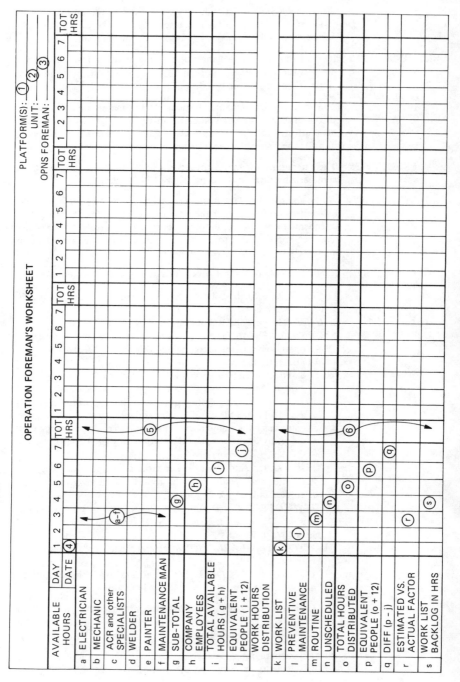

Exhibit 13-6A.

OPERATIONS FOREMAN'S WORKSHEET

PLATFORM(S): V2IL SMI 56 A1B
UNIT: TANGERINE
OPNS FOREMAN: BROWN/SMITH

AVAILABLE HOURS	DAY	1	2	3	4	5	6	7	TOT HRS
	DATE	9/1	9/2	9/3	9/4	9/5	9/6	9/7	
a ELECTRICIAN		12	12	12	12	12	12	12	84
b MECHANIC		8	12	-	-	-	-	-	20
c ACR and other SPECIALISTS		-	-	-	-	-	-	-	-
d WELDER		-	-	-	-	-	-	-	-
e PAINTER		-	-	-	-	-	-	-	-
f MAINTENANCE MAN		12	12	12	-	-	-	-	36
g SUB-TOTAL		32	36	24	12	12	12	12	140
h COMPANY EMPLOYEES		201	193	204	215	287	204	204	1475
i TOTAL AVAILABLE HOURS (g+h)		233	229	228	216	277	216	216	1615
j EQUIVALENT PEOPLE (i÷12)		19.4	19.1	19.0	18.0	18.9	18.0	18.0	19.2
WORK HOURS DISTRIBUTION									
k WORK LIST		74	82	50	78	87	74	72	517
l PREVENTIVE MAINTENANCE		2	-	-	10	2	-	13	27
m ROUTINE		58	58	58	58	63	58	58	411
n UNSCHEDULED		40	40	66	32	0	71	10	263
o TOTAL HOURS DISTRIBUTED		174	180	174	178	152	207	153	1218
p EQUIVALENT PEOPLE (o÷12)		14.5	15.0	14.5	14.8	12.7	17.3	12.8	14.5
q DIFF (p−j)		+4.9	+4.1	+4.5	+3.2	+6.2	+4.9	+5.2	+4.7
r ESTIMATED VS. ACTUAL FACTOR		83%	82%	87%	84%	74%	81%	84%	83%
s WORK LIST BACKLOG IN HRS		1540	1481	1468	1488	1511	1297	1225	1476

Exhibit 13-6B.

k. *WORK LIST.* From the Daily Work Reports, enter the total hours *actually* worked on Work List items for the day.

1. *PREVENTIVE MAINTENANCE.* From the Daily Work Reports, enter the total hours *actually* worked on preventive maintenance assignments for the day.

m. *ROUTINE.* Enter the predetermined number of hours assigned to the platform or work location for the accomplishment of routine work (see Daily Routine Activity Checklists for appropriate platforms).

n. *UNSCHEDULED.* From the Daily Work Reports, enter the total hours *actually* worked on assignments that were unscheduled (no item number).

o. *TOTAL HOURS DISTRIBUTED.* Total the entries for paragraphs k through n above, and enter.

p. *EQUIVALENT PEOPLE.* Divide the total hours distributed by 12 and enter the equivalent people reported at work for the day.

g. *DIFF.* Subtract the figure in paragraph p, above, from the figure in paragraph j, above, and enter the ($\pm$) result.

r. *ESTIMATED VS ACTUAL FIGURE.* From the Work List, total the estimated and actual hours on jobs completed that day. Divide the total estimated hours by the total actual hours to determine the *estimated-vs-actual factor* (entered as a percentage).

s. *WORK LIST BACKLOG IN HOURS.* On a daily basis, calculate and enter the current backlog in estimated hours for the platforms or work locations. The source is the Work List. As the operations foreman goes through the hitch, he subtracts the estimated hours for the jobs that are completed each day from the Work List Backlog in hours. Note that these hours in Backlog will change when the operations foreman conducts his weekly inspection of the platform. He adds estimated hours to the Backlog when this occurs.

6. *TOT HRS.* Summarize the total distributed hours for the hitch in each work category, and total. Note that for equivalent people for the hitch, total distributed hours are divided by 84 hours (7 days × 12 hours per day).

The estimated-vs.-actual factor is calculated for the entire week. Total the estimated hours on completed jobs for the week; total the actual hours used to complete those jobs. Divide the total estimated hours by the total actual hours. The resulting percentage is the estimated-vs-actual factor for the week. Note in the example that 517 actual hours were spent on Work List items. By checking the Work List the operations foreman can determine that 429 total estimated hours actually took 517 hours to complete:

$$429(\text{est hr}) \div 517 \,(\text{act hr}) = .829, \text{ or } 83\%$$

Divide the Work List Backlog in hours for the seventh day of the hitch by the weekly estimated-vs-actual hours factor (paragraph above) to adjust the Work List Backlog for the coming week. As shown in the example, 1225 Work List Backlog hours (shown on the seventh day) is divided by 83% (the weekly Est-vs-Act Hr Factor) to result in the beginning backlog (adjusted) for the next week:

1225 (Work List Backlog hr) ÷ .83 (i.e., 83%) = 1476 adjusted Backlog
hours to begin the next
week.

WEEKLY MANAGEMENT REPORT

PURPOSE   To provide the production superintendents and the division manager with timely and concise information on the weekly accomplishments of the units and the division, as a whole. Weekly monitoring will, in time, provide valuable information on trends as it relates to optimum crew levels.

RESPONSIBILITIES   The operations foreman provides a copy of his *Operations Foreman's Worksheet(s)* weekly through the production foreman to the production superintendent and the Maintenance Support Group.

The *Maintenance Support Group,* using the information provided on the Operation Foreman's Worksheets, compiles a Weekly Management Report by unit for the production superintendent. Additionally, using the production superintendent's Weekly Management Reports, he prepares a consolidated *Weekly Management Report,* covering the division's units for the division manager.

FREQUENCY   The Weekly Management Reports are quarterly, updated weekly.

DISTRIBUTION   Each production superintendent receives his unit's Weekly Management Report; the division manager receives his Weekly Management Report and copies of the individual units' Weekly Management Reports.

PREPARATION   Refer to the blank control (Exs. 13.7a and b) keyed to the following:

1. *QTR.* Enter the appropriate quarter of the year.
2. *YEAR.* Enter the current year.
3. *UNIT.* Enter the unit for which the report is made; in the case of the division report, enter TOTAL DIV.
4. *PREV QTR.* Enter the average, in each category, from the previous quarter's report.
5. *WEEK (preprinted).* The number of the week in the quarter.
6. *DATE.* Enter the week ending date. For the purpose of this report, the cut-off day for the week is Wednesday. This is done as the majority of the units' personnel operate on a 7 and 7 basis, and the majority of the operations foremen change on Wednesdays.

Note: Paragraphs a through s, below, are identical to paragraphs a through s, *Operations Foreman's Worksheet.* They are repeated here only to show the checks on the entries that can be made by the production superintendent. (Source: Each Worksheet's total weekly hours).

WEEKLY MANAGEMENT REPORT
OFFSHORE WEST DIVISION

QTR: ①   YEAR: ②
UNIT: ③

AVAILABLE HOURS	WEEK DATE	PREV QTR	1	2	3	4	5	6	7	8	9	10	11	12	13	QTR AVER
a	ELECTRICIAN	④	⑥													
b	MECHANIC															
c	ACR and other SPECIALISTS															
d	WELDER															
e	PAINTER															⑦
f	MAINTENANCE MAN															
g	SUB-TOTAL				⑨											
h	COMPANY EMPLOYEES					ⓗ										
i	TOTAL AVAILABLE HOURS (g + h)						ⓘ									
j	EQUIVALENT PEOPLE (i ÷ 84)								ⓙ							
	WORK HOURS DISTRIBUTION															
k	WORK LIST															
l	PREVENTIVE MAINTENANCE															
m	ROUTINE															⑦
n	UNSCHEDULED															
o	TOTAL HOURS DISTRIBUTED		ⓞ													
p	EQUIVALENT PEOPLE (o ÷ 84)			ⓟ												
q	DIFFERENCE (p − j)				ⓠ											
r	ESTIMATED VS. ACTUAL FACTOR					ⓡ										
s	WORK LIST BACKLOG IN HOURS						ⓢ									

Exhibit 13-7A.

WEEKLY MANAGEMENT REPORT
OFFSHORE WEST DIVISION

QTR: _____ YEAR: _____
UNIT: TANGERINE

AVAILABLE HOURS	WEEK / DATE	PREV QTR	1 7/6	2 7/13	3 7/20	4 7/27	5 8/3	6 8/10	7 8/17	8 8/24	9 8/31	10 9/7	11 9/14	12 9/21	13 9/28	QTR AVER
a	ELECTRICIAN										231	252				
b	MECHANIC										48	63				
c	ACR and other SPECIALISTS										—	12				
d	WELDER										—	12				
e	PAINTER										—	—				
f	MAINTENANCE MAN										48	72				
g	SUB-TOTAL										327	411				
h	COMPANY EMPLOYEES										4463	4425				
i	TOTAL AVAILABLE HOURS (g + h)										4790	4836				
j	EQUIVALENT PEOPLE (i ÷ 84)										57.0	57.6				
	WORK HOURS DISTRIBUTION															
k	WORK LIST										1610	1532				
l	PREVENTIVE MAINTENANCE										57	76				
m	ROUTINE										1212	1212				
n	UNSCHEDULED										814	623				
o	TOTAL HOURS DISTRIBUTED										3693	3443				
p	EQUIVALENT PEOPLE (o ÷ 84)										44.0	41.0				
q	DIFFERENCE (p – j)										+13.0	+16.6				
r	ESTIMATED VS. ACTUAL FACTOR										81%	82%				
s	WORK LIST BACKLOG IN HOURS										4563	4428				

Exhibit 13-7B.

a.–f. Contractor Employee Work Classifications. Listed under paragraphs a through f, are the total contractor hours worked during the week by work classification.

g. *SUBTOTAL.* Add entries in paragraphs a through f, and enter the sum.

h. *EMPLOYEES.* Total company employee hours for the week.

i. *TOTAL AVAILABLE HOURS.* Total entries in paragraghs g and h and enter the sum.

j. *EQUIVALENT PEOPLE.* Divide the total available hours by 84 to determine the total equivalent people for the week.

k.–n. *WORK LIST, PREVENTIVE MAINTENANCE, ROUTINE, AND UNSCHEDULED.* Enter the hours recorded in each of these blocks for the week.

o. *TOTAL HOURS DISTRIBUTED.* Total paragraphs k through n, and enter the sum.

p. *EQUIVALENT PEOPLE.* Divide the total hours distributed by 84 to determine the total equivalent people reported at work for the week.

q. *DIFF.* Subtract the figure in paragraph p from the figure in paragraph j, and enter the ($\pm$) result.

r. *ESTIMATED-VS-ACTUAL FACTOR.* A couple of steps are necessary to derive the Estimated-vs-Actual Factor for the unit and the division:

List the operations foremen for the unit (or units in the division), their Work List hours (paragraph k), and their individual Est-vs-Act Factor. Example:

OPERATIONS FOREMAN	WORK LIST HOURS	EST-VS- ACT FACTOR	ESTIMATED HOURS
H. Jones	751	83%	
B. Smith	476	114%	
C. Davis	602	87%	
	1829		

Multiply the Work List Hours by the Est-vs-Act Factor to obtain the Estimated Hours completed for the week:

OPERATIONS FOREMAN	WORK LIST HOURS		EST-VS. ACT FACTOR		ESTIMATED HOURS
H. Jones	751	×	.83	=	623
B. Smith	476	×	1.14	=	543
C. Davis	602	×	.87	=	524
					1690

Total the Work List hours (Example: 1829); total the estimated hours (Example: 1690); for all operations foremen in the unit (or all units in the division).

Divide the total estimated hours by the total Work List hours. The resulting percentage is the Est-vs-Act Factor for the unit (division). Example:

1690 (tot est hr) ÷ 1829 (tot Work List Hr) = .924, or 92%

    s. *WORK LIST BACKLOG IN HOURS.* Enter the adjusted Work List Backlog as recorded on the Worksheets. This figure represents the total hours in backlog for the coming week.

7. *QTR AVER.* Determine the average for the quarter, then enter here and in the first column (PREV QTR) of the succeeding Weekly Management Report.

Paragraphs a through i are totaled and divided by 13 weeks. Note: Do not include the Previous Quarters figures in the calculations.

Paragraph j is determined by dividing the Total Available Hours for the quarter by 1,092 (84 hrs/wk × 13 weeks).

Paragraphs k through o are totaled and divided by 13 weeks.

Paragraph p is determined by dividing the total hours distributed for the quarter by 1092, as above.

Paragraph q is determined by subtracting the result in paragraph p, above, from the result in paragraph j, above.

Paragraph r is determined as outlined in paragraph r, above. Divide the average total estimated hours by the average total Work List hours.

Paragraph s is not determined. It is the final Backlog in hours recorded in the 13th week of the quarter.

CONCLUSION

In this particular history, the principles of good management are employed to the point of involvement of all personnel.

- The first-line foreman plans, assigns, and does follow-up.
- The people under him are aware of the requirements and actually report their work.
- The production foreman follows up with the first-line foreman.
- The superintendent follows up with the production foreman and reports upward to the division head.

With the enthusiastic support of upper management, the full involvement of all levels of middle management, and provision of first-line supervision with the tools and training to enable it to do its job better, all companies can improve their profits in the same manner.

Index

Index